The AMAZING SPIDER-MAN

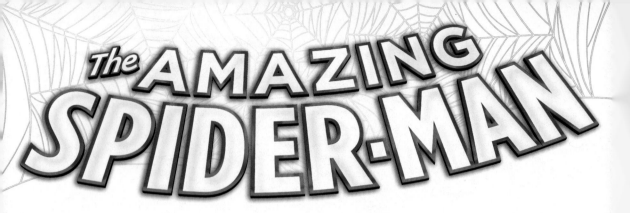

The AMAZING SPIDER-MAN

AMAZING GRACE

JOSE MOLINA
WRITER

ISSUE #1.1
ARTIST/COVER: SIMONE BIANCHI
COLOR ARTIST: ISRAEL SILVA
LETTERER: VC's JOE CARAMAGNA

ISSUE #1.2
ARTIST/COVER: SIMONE BIANCHI
COLOR ARTISTS: ISRAEL SILVA, JAVA TARTAGLIA, ANDRES MOSSA & MARTE GRACIA
LETTERER: VC's JOE CARAMAGNA

ISSUE #1.3
ARTIST/COVER: SIMONE BIANCHI
COLOR ARTISTS: ISRAEL SILVA & JAVA TARTAGLIA
LETTERER: VC's JOE CARAMAGNA

ISSUE #1.4
ARTISTS: SIMONE BIANCHI & ANDREA BROCCARDO
COLOR ARTIST: DAVID CURIEL
LETTERER: VC's JOE CARAMAGNA
COVER ART: SIMONE BIANCHI

ISSUE #1.5
PENCILERS: SIMONE BIANCHI & RAYMUND BERMUDEZ
INKER: LORENZO RUGGIERO
COLOR ARTIST: DAVID CURIEL
LETTERER: VC's CLAYTON COWLES
COVER ART: SIMONE BIANCHI

ISSUE #1.6
ARTISTS: SIMONE BIANCHI & ANDREA BROCCARDO
COLOR ARTISTS: DAVID CURIEL & MATT YACKEY
LETTERER: VC's JOE SABINO
COVER ART: GIUSEPPE CAMUNCOLI & DAVID CURIEL

DEVIN LEWIS
ASSISTANT EDITOR

NICK LOWE
EDITOR

SPIDER-MAN CREATED BY
STAN LEE & STEVE DITKO

COLLECTION EDITOR: **JENNIFER GRÜNWALD**
ASSOCIATE EDITOR: **SARAH BRUNSTAD**
EDITOR, SPECIAL PROJECTS: **MARK D. BEAZLEY**

VP, PRODUCTION & SPECIAL PROJECTS: **JEFF YOUNGQUIST**
SVP PRINT, SALES & MARKETING: **DAVID GABRIEL**
BOOK DESIGNER: **ADAM DEL RE**

EDITOR IN CHIEF: **AXEL ALONSO**
CHIEF CREATIVE OFFICER: **JOE QUESADA**
PUBLISHER: **DAN BUCKLEY**
EXECUTIVE PRODUCER: **ALAN FINE**

AMAZING SPIDER-MAN: AMAZING GRACE. Contains material originally published in magazine form as AMAZING SPIDER-MAN (2015) #1.1-1.6. First printing 2016. ISBN# 978-0-7851-9661-7. Published by MARVEL WORLDWIDE, INC., a subsidiary of MARVEL ENTERTAINMENT, LLC. OFFICE OF PUBLICATION: 135 West 50th Street, New York, NY 10020. **Printed in Canada.** ALAN FINE, President, Marvel Entertainment; DAN BUCKLEY, President, TV, Publishing & Brand Management; JOE QUESADA, Chief Creative Officer; TOM BREVOORT, SVP of Publishing; DAVID BOGART, SVP of Business Affairs & Operations, Publishing & Partnership; C.B. CEBULSKI, VP of Brand Management & Development, Asia; DAVID GABRIEL, SVP of Sales & Marketing, Publishing; JEFF YOUNGQUIST, VP of Production & Special Projects; DAN CARR, Executive Director of Publishing Technology; ALEX MORALES, Director of Publishing Operations; SUSAN CRESPI, Production Manager; STAN LEE, Chairman Emeritus. For information regarding advertising in Marvel Comics or on Marvel.com, please contact Vit DeBellis, Integrated Sales Manager, at vdebellis@marvel.com. For Marvel subscription inquiries, please call 888-511-5480. **Manufactured between 7/1/2016 and 8/10/2016 by SOLISCO PRINTERS, SCOTT, QC, CANADA.**

10 9 8 7 6 5 4 3 2 1

WHEN PETER PARKER WAS BITTEN BY A RADIOACTIVE SPIDER, HE GAINED THE PROPORTIONAL SPEED, STRENGTH AND AGILITY OF A SPIDER; ADHESIVE FINGERTIPS AND TOES; AND THE UNIQUE PRECOGNITIVE AWARENESS OF DANGER CALLED "SPIDER-SENSE"! AFTER LEARNING THAT WITH GREAT POWER THERE MUST ALSO COME GREAT RESPONSIBILITY, HE BECAME THE CRIMEFIGHTING SUPER HERO CALLED...

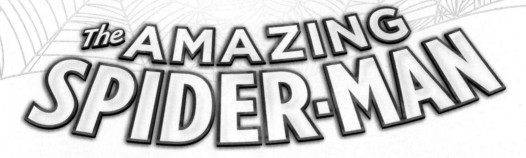

The AMAZING SPIDER-MAN

PETER PARKER HAS GONE GLOBAL! HIS TECHNOLOGY COMPANY, PARKER INDUSTRIES, HAS FINALLY BECOME A MAJOR PLAYER IN THE GLOBAL MARKETPLACE. EVEN THOUGH HE'S GOT OFFICES AROUND THE WORLD, SOMETIMES THE WALL-CRAWLING WEB-SLINGER LIKES TO SPEND TIME IN A CLOSER, FRIENDLIER NEIGHBORHOOD... ESPECIALLY DURING THE HOLIDAYS!

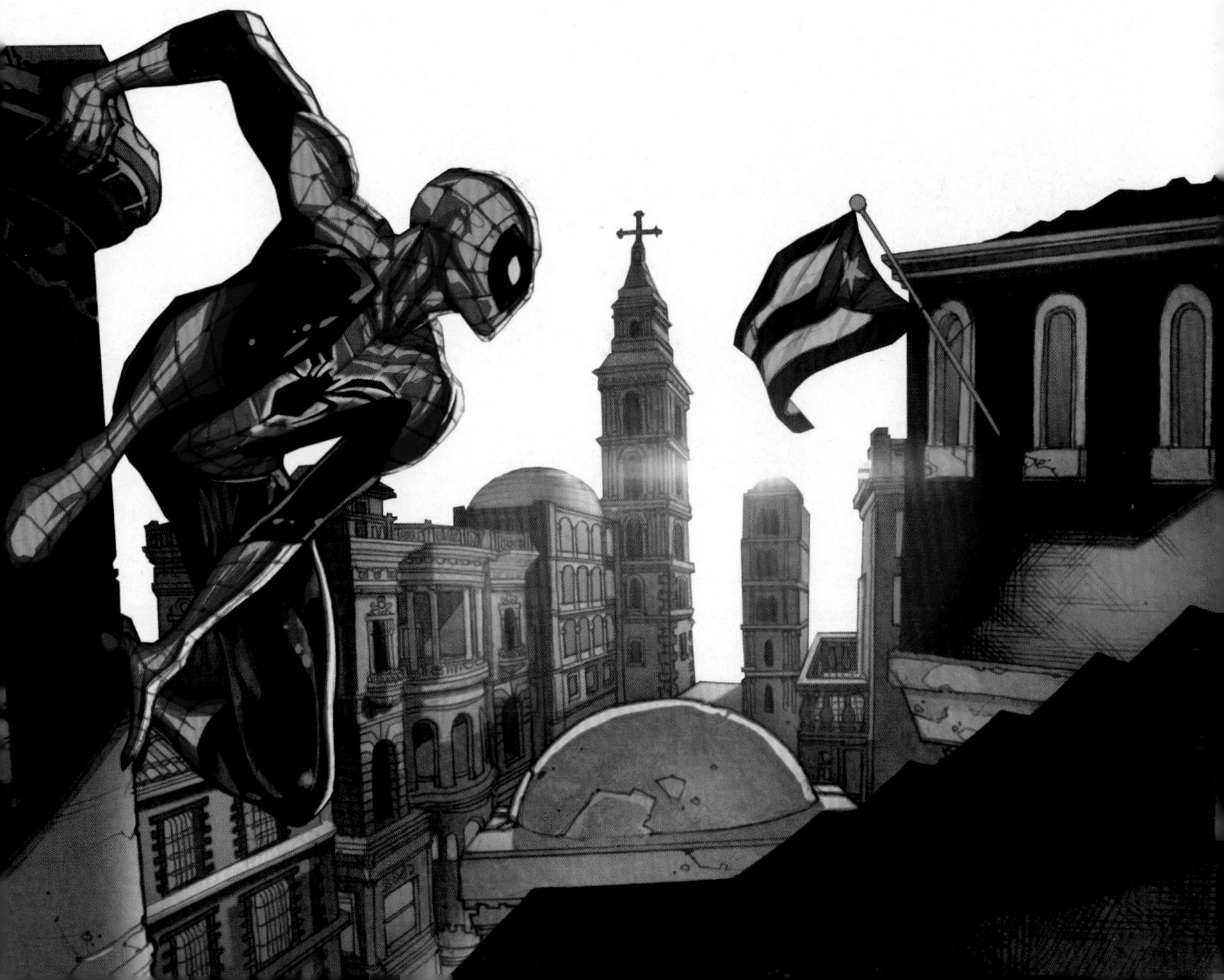

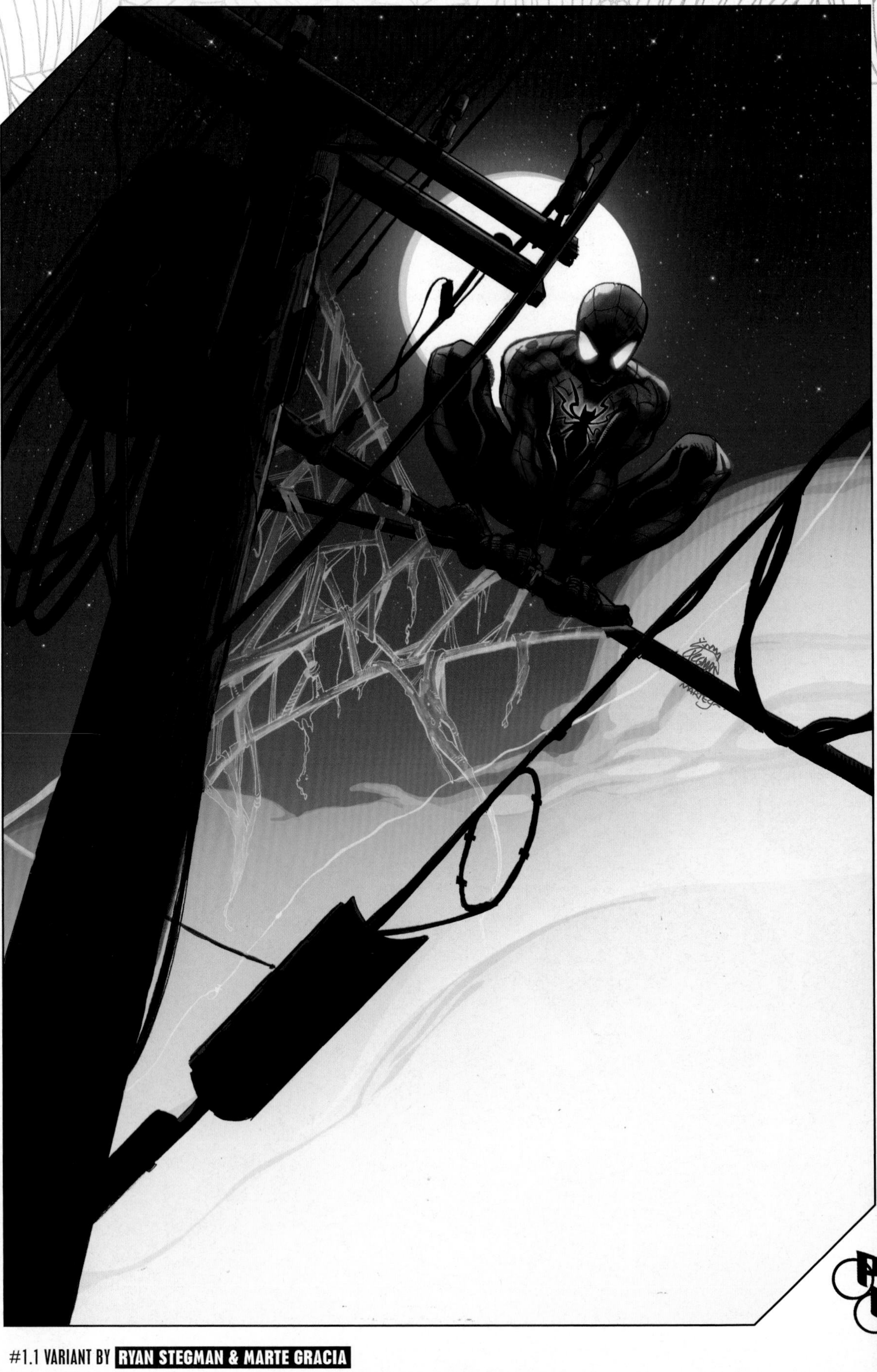

#1.1 VARIANT BY **RYAN STEGMAN & MARTE GRACIA**

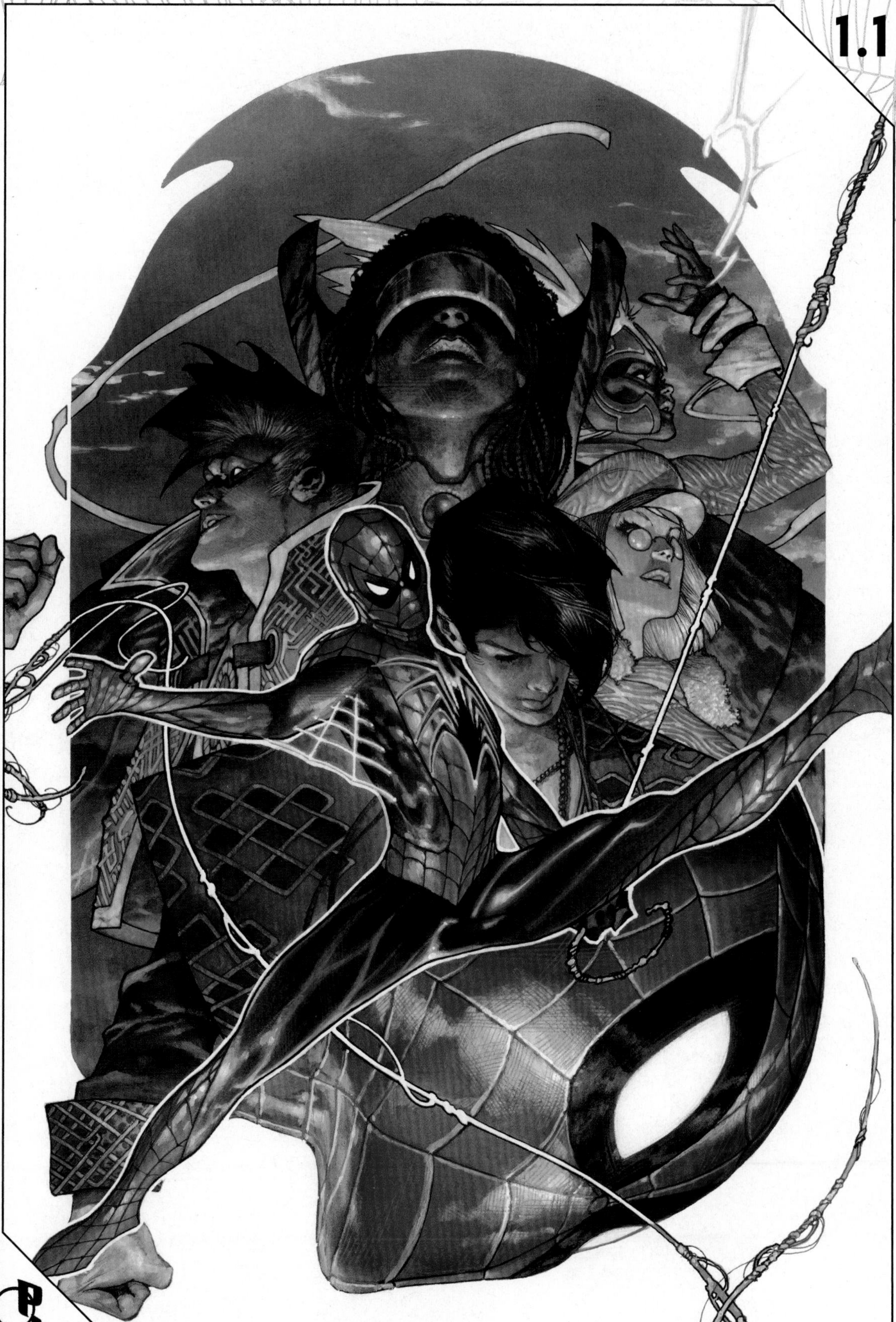

"A WRETCH LIKE ME"

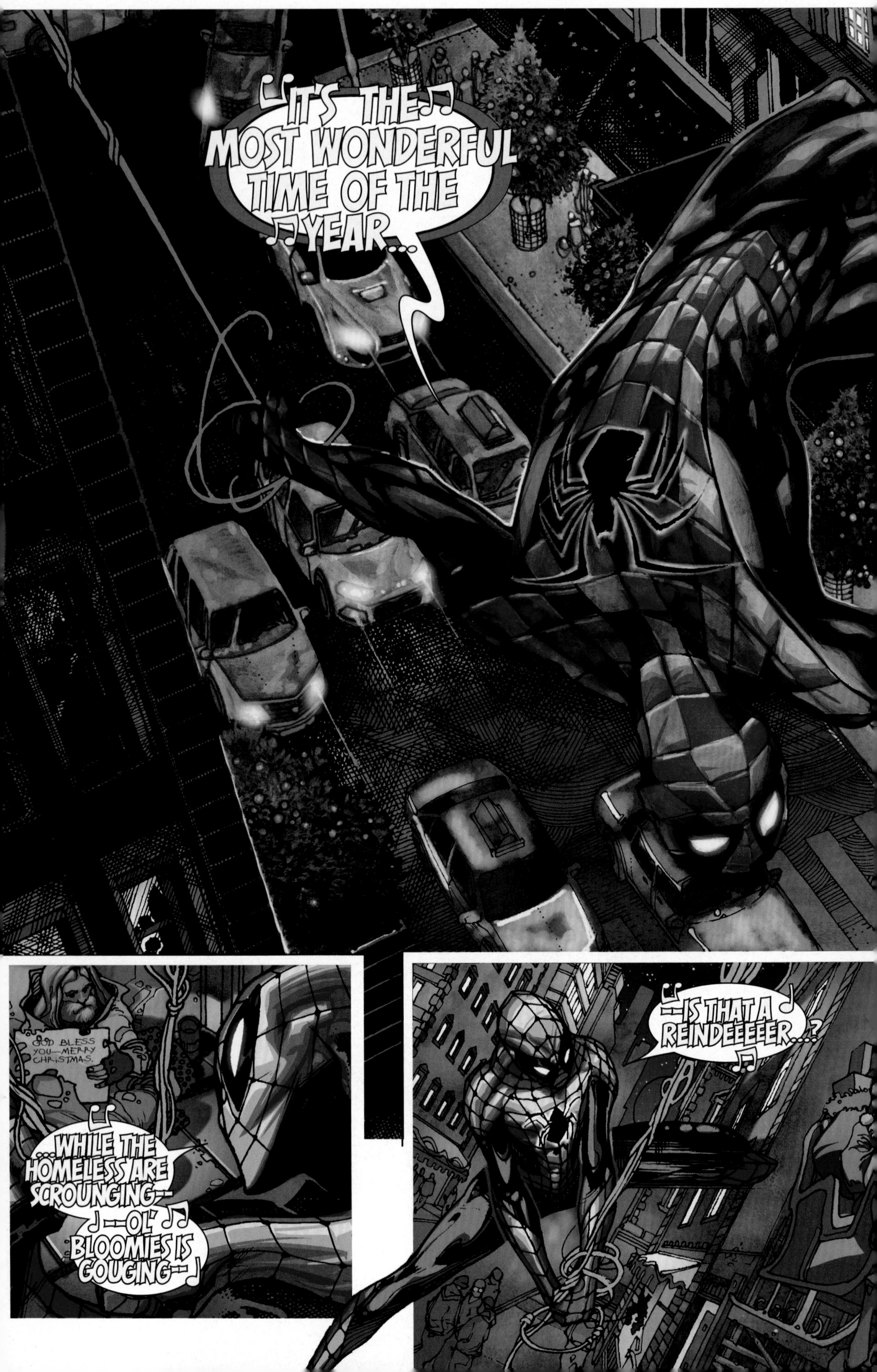
IT'S THE MOST WONDERFUL TIME OF THE YEAR...
GOD BLESS YOU—MERRY CHRISTMAS.
...WHILE THE HOMELESS ARE SCROUNGING-
--OL' BLOOMIES IS GOUGING--
--IS THAT A REINDEEEEER...?

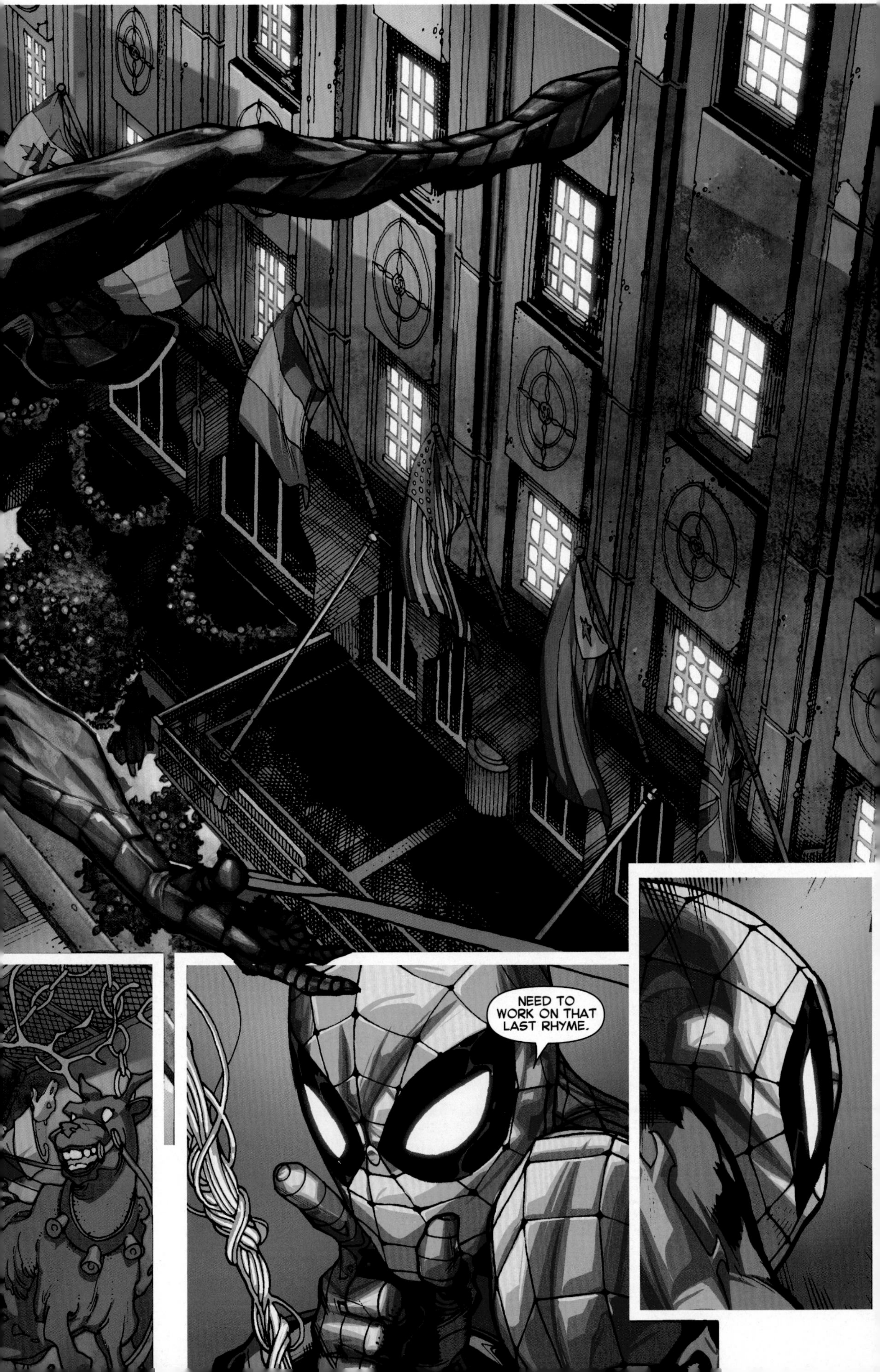
NEED TO WORK ON THAT LAST RHYME.

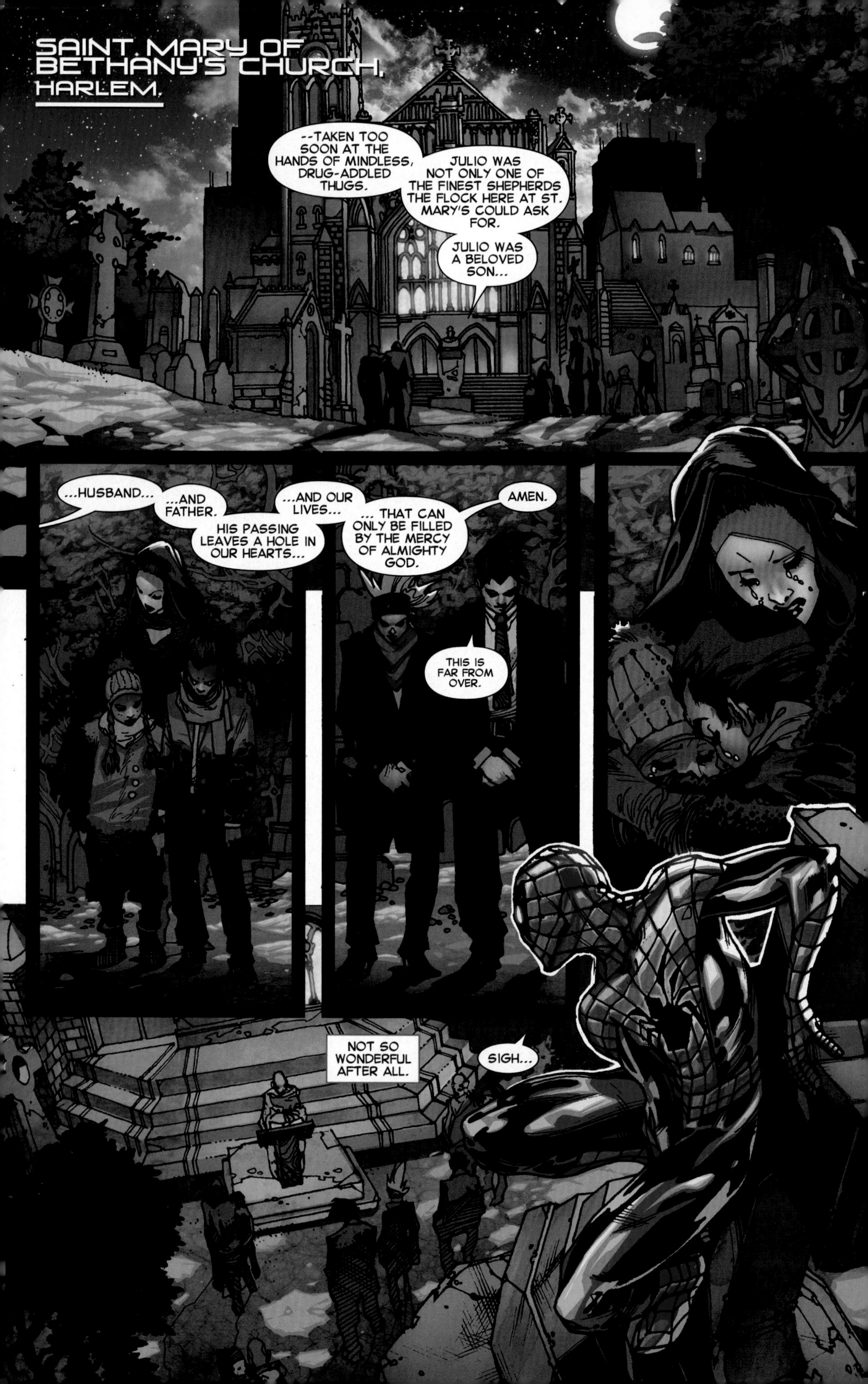
SAINT MARY OF BETHANY'S CHURCH, HARLEM.
--TAKEN TOO SOON AT THE HANDS OF MINDLESS, DRUG-ADDLED THUGS.
JULIO WAS NOT ONLY ONE OF THE FINEST SHEPHERDS THE FLOCK HERE AT ST. MARY'S COULD ASK FOR.
JULIO WAS A BELOVED SON...
...HUSBAND...
...AND FATHER.
HIS PASSING LEAVES A HOLE IN OUR HEARTS...
...AND OUR LIVES...
... THAT CAN ONLY BE FILLED BY THE MERCY OF ALMIGHTY GOD.
AMEN.
THIS IS FAR FROM OVER.
NOT SO WONDERFUL AFTER ALL.
SIGH...

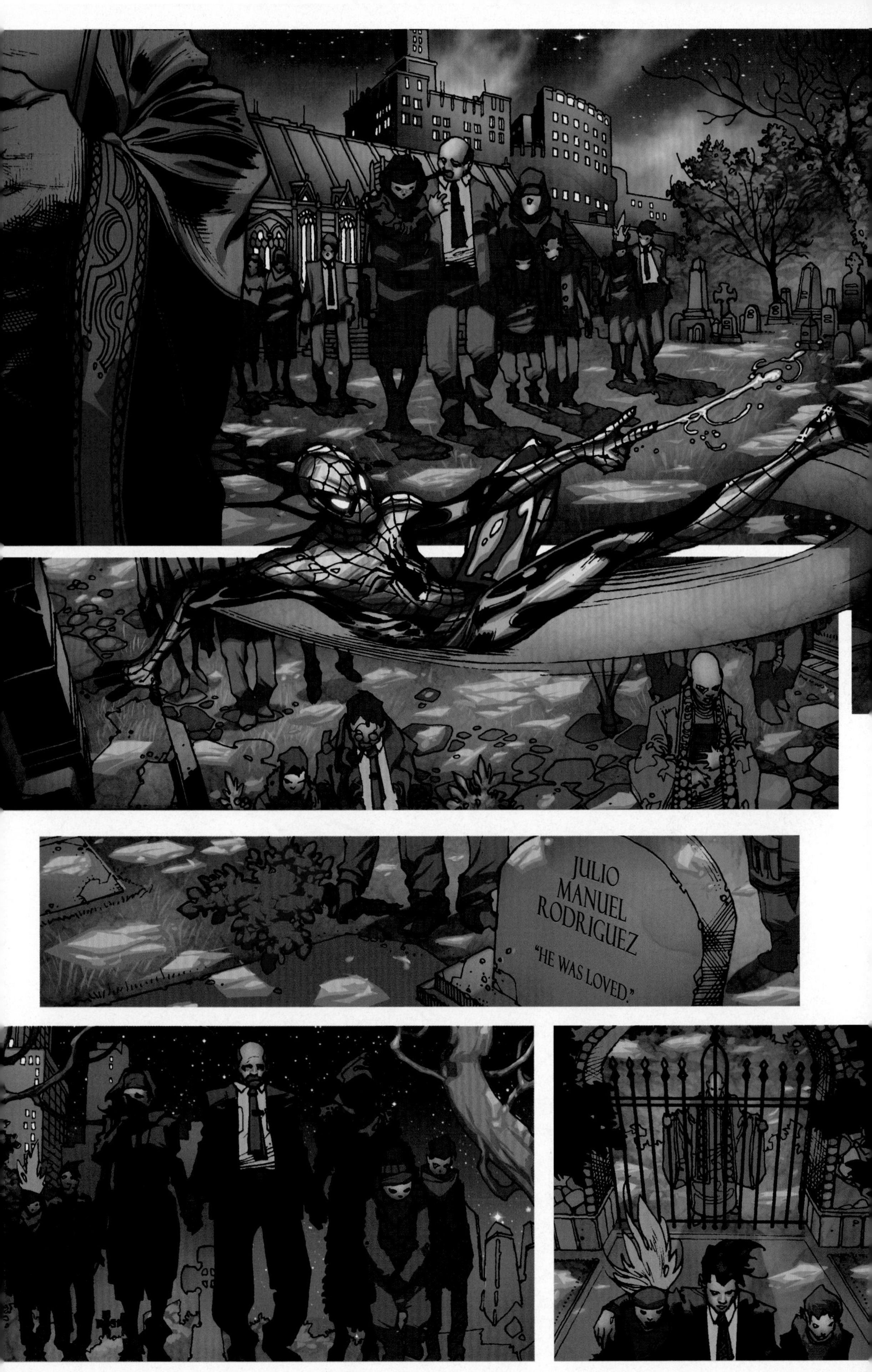
JULIO
MANUEL
RODRIGUEZ
"HE WAS LOVED."

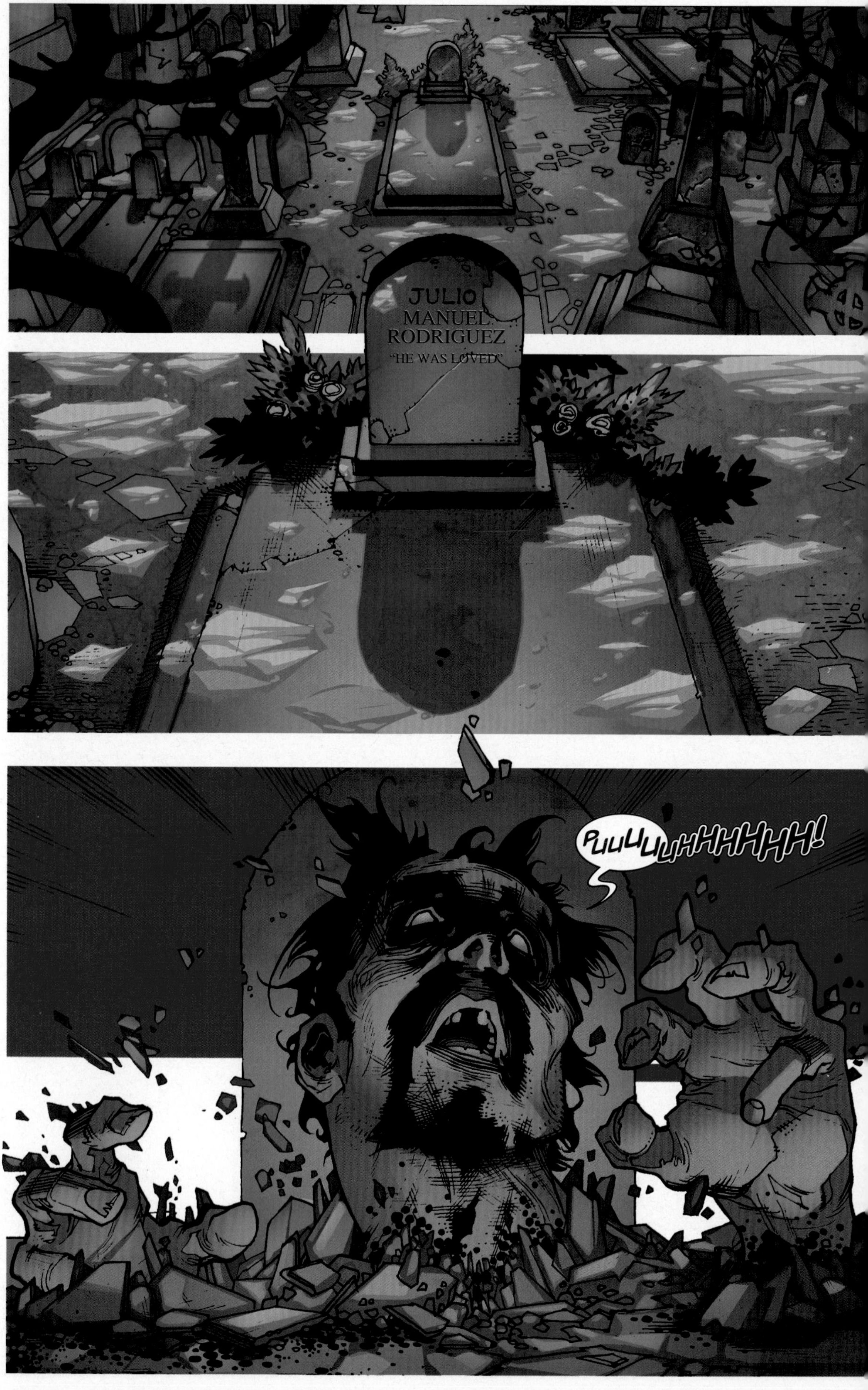
JULIO
MANUEL
RODRIGUEZ
"HE WAS LOVED"
PUUUUUHHHHHH!

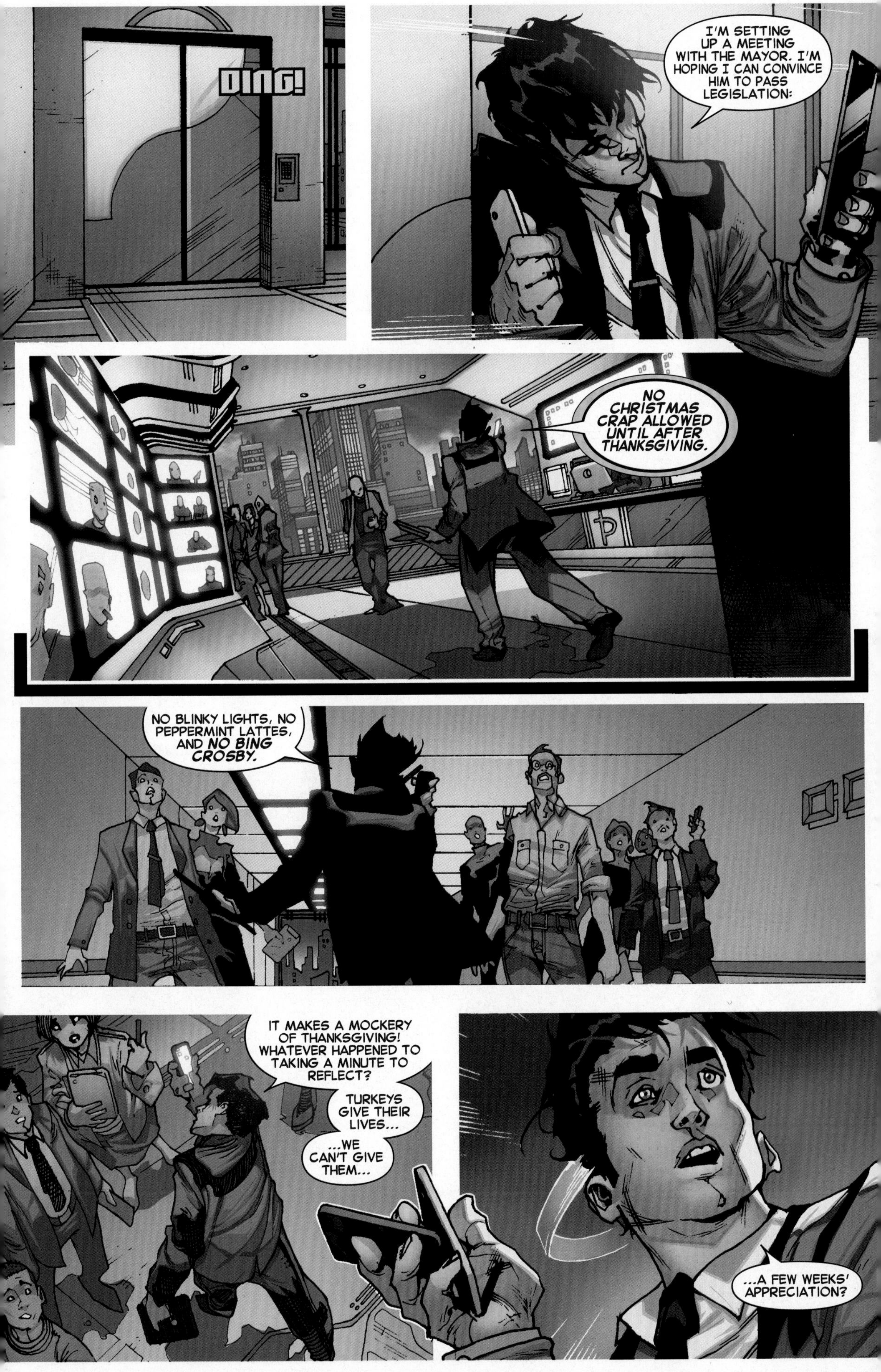
DING!
I'M SETTING UP A MEETING WITH THE MAYOR. I'M HOPING I CAN CONVINCE HIM TO PASS LEGISLATION:
NO CHRISTMAS CRAP ALLOWED UNTIL AFTER THANKSGIVING.
NO BLINKY LIGHTS, NO PEPPERMINT LATTES, AND NO BING CROSBY.
IT MAKES A MOCKERY OF THANKSGIVING! WHATEVER HAPPENED TO TAKING A MINUTE TO REFLECT?
TURKEYS GIVE THEIR LIVES...
...WE CAN'T GIVE THEM...
...A FEW WEEKS' APPRECIATION?

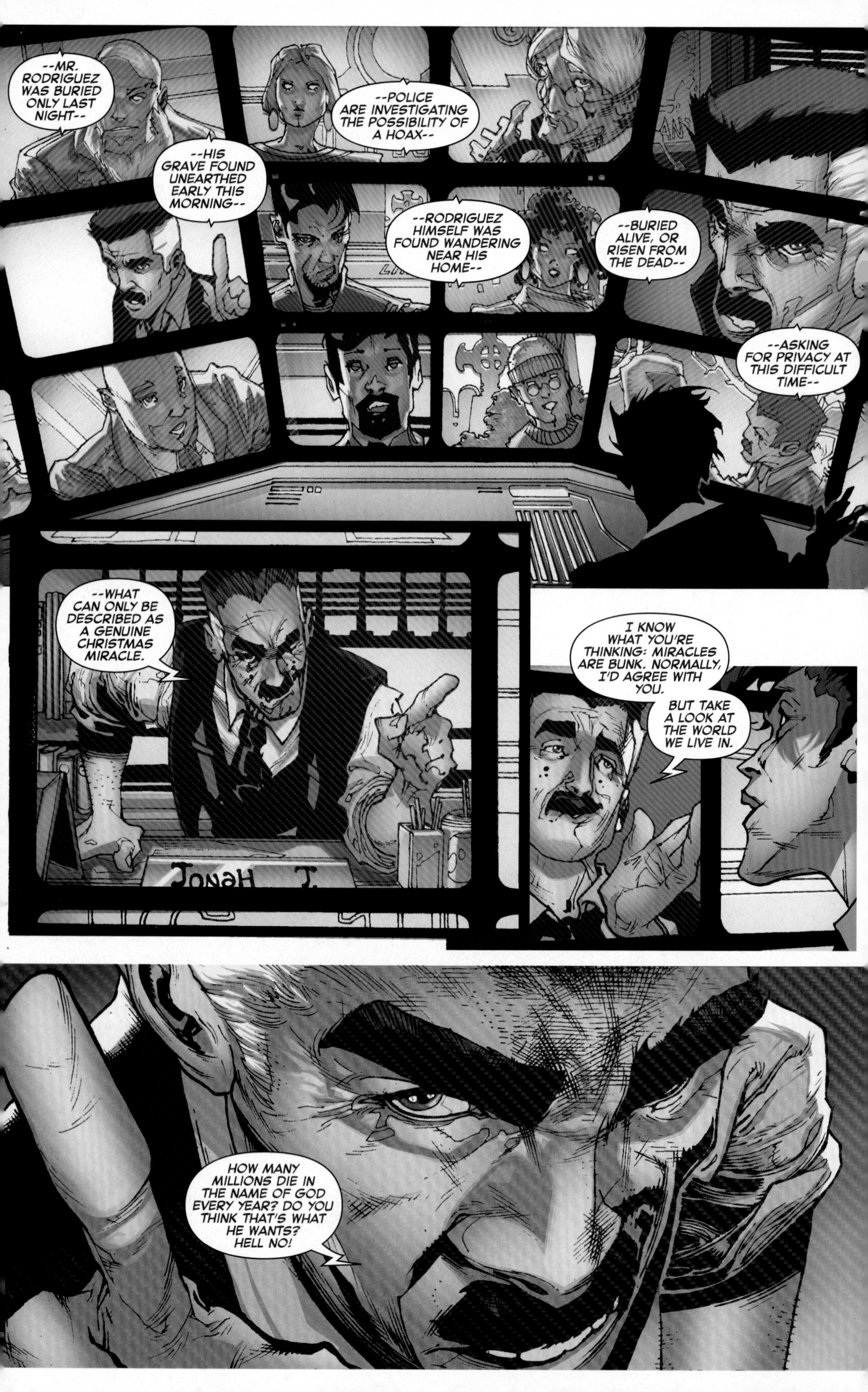

--MR. RODRIGUEZ WAS BURIED ONLY LAST NIGHT--
--POLICE ARE INVESTIGATING THE POSSIBILITY OF A HOAX--
--HIS GRAVE FOUND UNEARTHED EARLY THIS MORNING--
--RODRIGUEZ HIMSELF WAS FOUND WANDERING NEAR HIS HOME--
--BURIED ALIVE, OR RISEN FROM THE DEAD--
--ASKING FOR PRIVACY AT THIS DIFFICULT TIME--
--WHAT CAN ONLY BE DESCRIBED AS A GENUINE CHRISTMAS MIRACLE.
JONAH J.
I KNOW WHAT YOU'RE THINKING: MIRACLES ARE BUNK. NORMALLY, I'D AGREE WITH YOU.
BUT TAKE A LOOK AT THE WORLD WE LIVE IN.
HOW MANY MILLIONS DIE IN THE NAME OF GOD EVERY YEAR? DO YOU THINK THAT'S WHAT HE WANTS? HELL NO!

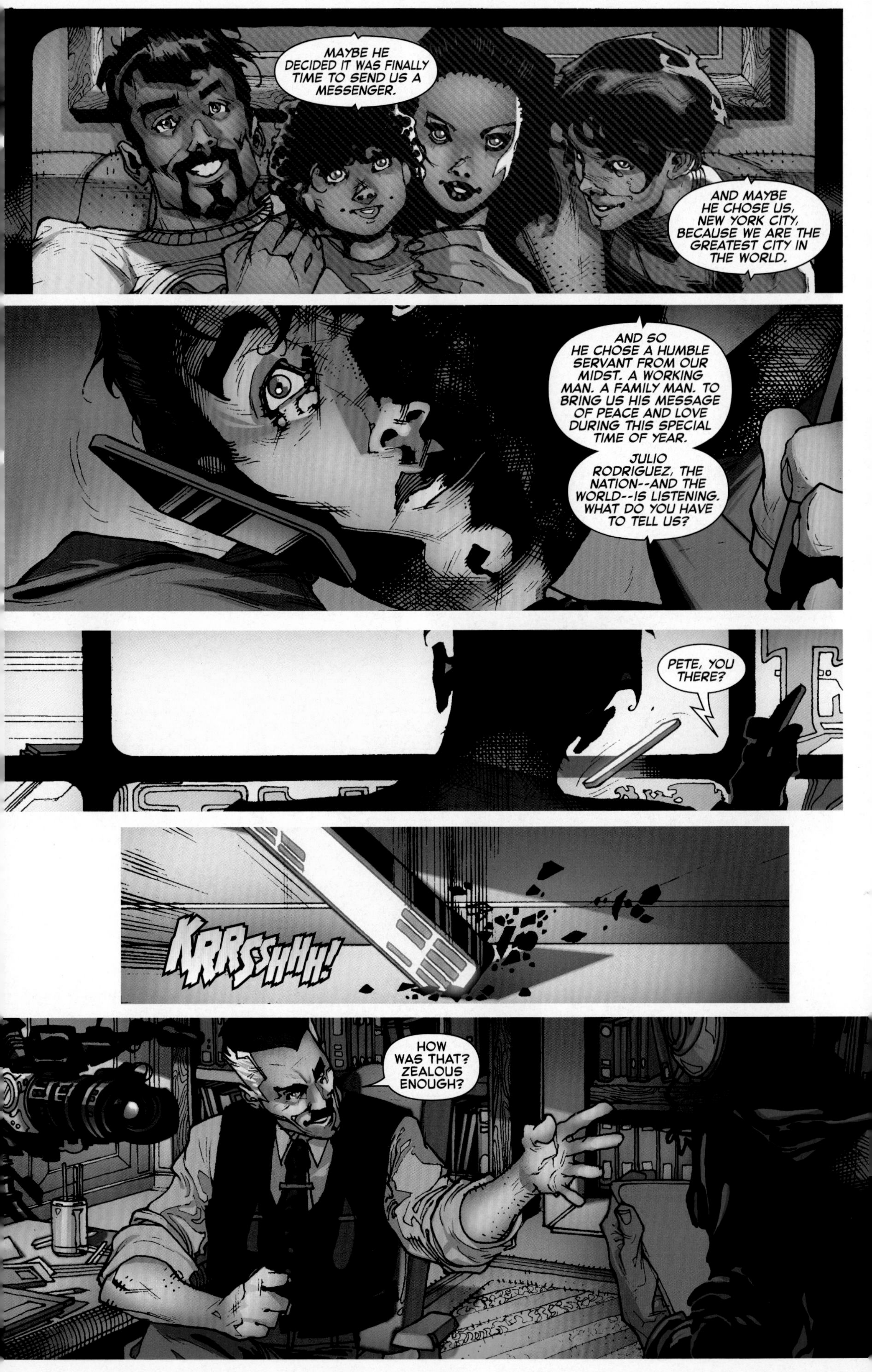
MAYBE HE DECIDED IT WAS FINALLY TIME TO SEND US A MESSENGER.
AND MAYBE HE CHOSE US, NEW YORK CITY, BECAUSE WE ARE THE GREATEST CITY IN THE WORLD.
AND SO HE CHOSE A HUMBLE SERVANT FROM OUR MIDST. A WORKING MAN. A FAMILY MAN. TO BRING US HIS MESSAGE OF PEACE AND LOVE DURING THIS SPECIAL TIME OF YEAR.
JULIO RODRIGUEZ, THE NATION--AND THE WORLD--IS LISTENING. WHAT DO YOU HAVE TO TELL US?
PETE, YOU THERE?
KRRSSHHH!
HOW WAS THAT? ZEALOUS ENOUGH?

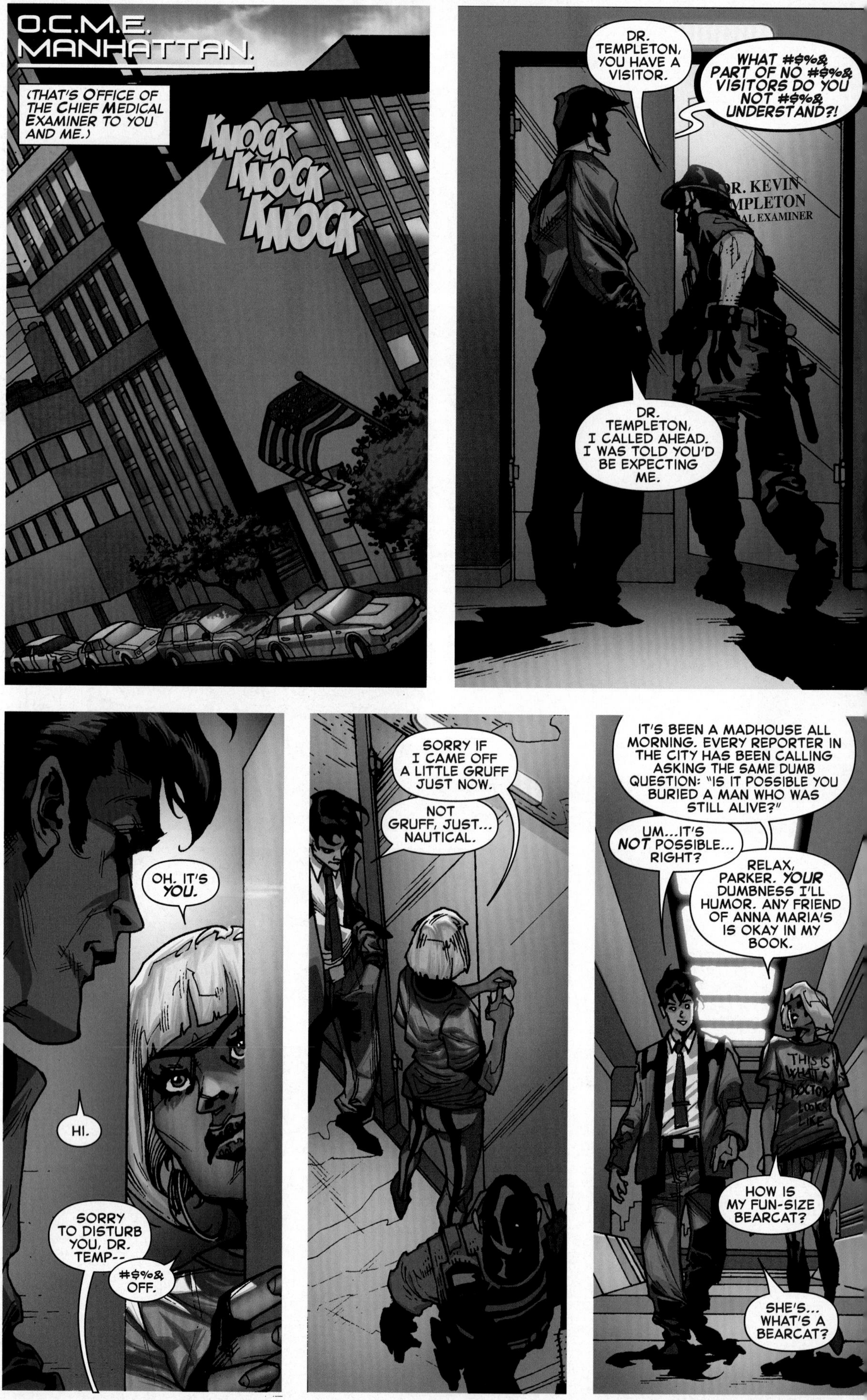
O.C.M.E. MANHATTAN.
(THAT'S OFFICE OF THE CHIEF MEDICAL EXAMINER TO YOU AND ME.)
KNOCK KNOCK KNOCK
DR. TEMPLETON, YOU HAVE A VISITOR.
WHAT #$%& PART OF NO #$%& VISITORS DO YOU NOT #$%& UNDERSTAND?!
DR. KEVIN TEMPLETON
MEDICAL EXAMINER
DR. TEMPLETON, I CALLED AHEAD. I WAS TOLD YOU'D BE EXPECTING ME.
OH. IT'S YOU.
HI.
SORRY TO DISTURB YOU, DR. TEMP--
#$%& OFF.
SORRY IF I CAME OFF A LITTLE GRUFF JUST NOW.
NOT GRUFF, JUST... NAUTICAL.
IT'S BEEN A MADHOUSE ALL MORNING. EVERY REPORTER IN THE CITY HAS BEEN CALLING ASKING THE SAME DUMB QUESTION: "IS IT POSSIBLE YOU BURIED A MAN WHO WAS STILL ALIVE?"
UM...IT'S NOT POSSIBLE... RIGHT?
RELAX, PARKER. YOUR DUMBNESS I'LL HUMOR. ANY FRIEND OF ANNA MARIA'S IS OKAY IN MY BOOK.
THIS IS WHAT A DOCTOR LOOKS LIKE
HOW IS MY FUN-SIZE BEARCAT?
SHE'S... WHAT'S A BEARCAT?

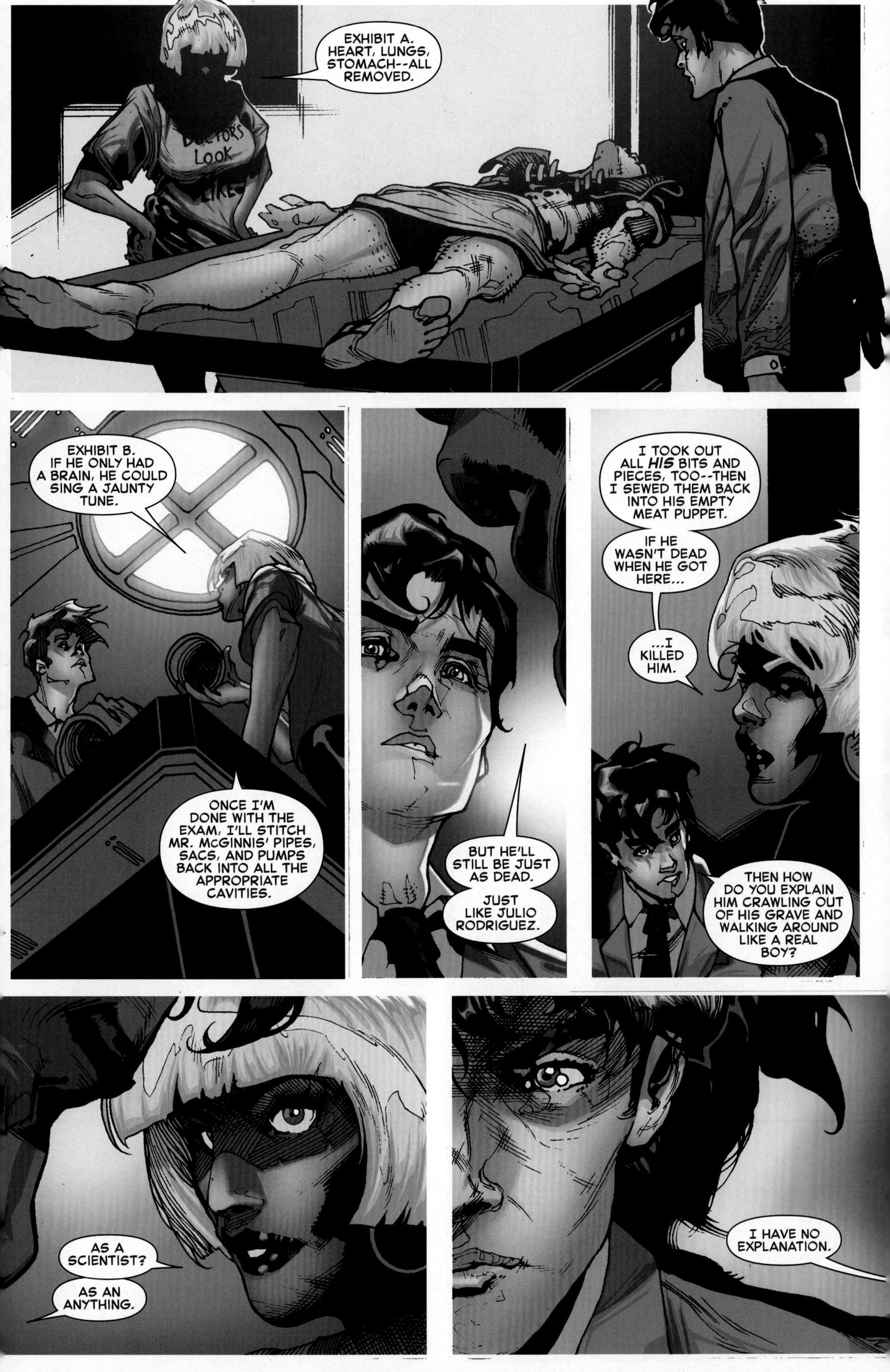

EXHIBIT A. HEART, LUNGS, STOMACH--ALL REMOVED.
DOCTORS LOOK LIKE
EXHIBIT B. IF HE ONLY HAD A BRAIN, HE COULD SING A JAUNTY TUNE.
ONCE I'M DONE WITH THE EXAM, I'LL STITCH MR. McGINNIS' PIPES, SACS, AND PUMPS BACK INTO ALL THE APPROPRIATE CAVITIES.
BUT HE'LL STILL BE JUST AS DEAD.
JUST LIKE JULIO RODRIGUEZ.
I TOOK OUT ALL *HIS* BITS AND PIECES, TOO--THEN I SEWED THEM BACK INTO HIS EMPTY MEAT PUPPET.
IF HE WASN'T DEAD WHEN HE GOT HERE...
...I KILLED HIM.
THEN HOW DO YOU EXPLAIN HIM CRAWLING OUT OF HIS GRAVE AND WALKING AROUND LIKE A REAL BOY?
AS A SCIENTIST?
AS AN ANYTHING.
I HAVE NO EXPLANATION.

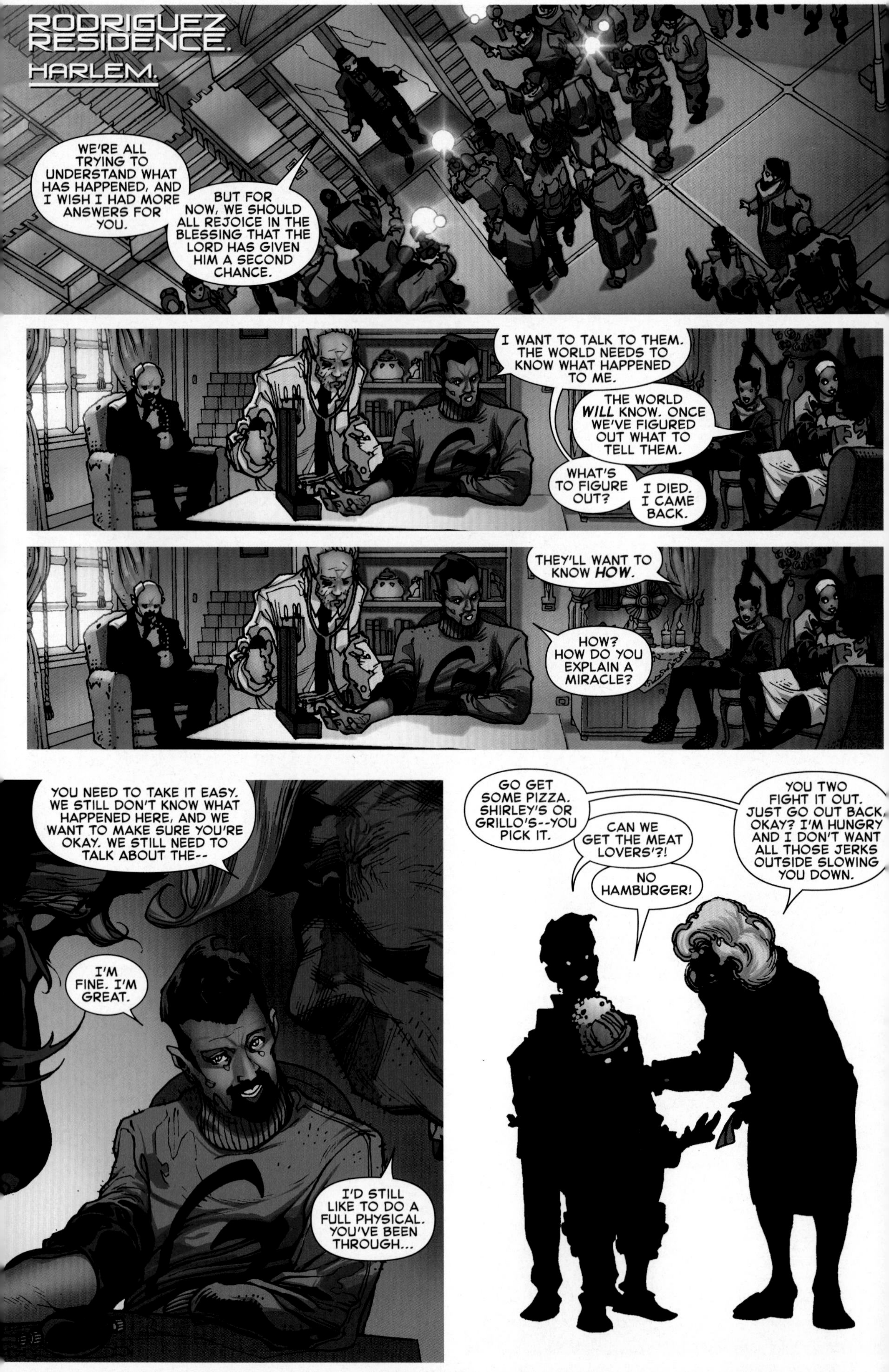

RODRIGUEZ RESIDENCE.
HARLEM.
WE'RE ALL TRYING TO UNDERSTAND WHAT HAS HAPPENED, AND I WISH I HAD MORE ANSWERS FOR YOU.
BUT FOR NOW, WE SHOULD ALL REJOICE IN THE BLESSING THAT THE LORD HAS GIVEN HIM A SECOND CHANCE.
I WANT TO TALK TO THEM. THE WORLD NEEDS TO KNOW WHAT HAPPENED TO ME.
THE WORLD WILL KNOW. ONCE WE'VE FIGURED OUT WHAT TO TELL THEM.
WHAT'S TO FIGURE OUT?
I DIED. I CAME BACK.
THEY'LL WANT TO KNOW HOW.
HOW? HOW DO YOU EXPLAIN A MIRACLE?
YOU NEED TO TAKE IT EASY. WE STILL DON'T KNOW WHAT HAPPENED HERE, AND WE WANT TO MAKE SURE YOU'RE OKAY. WE STILL NEED TO TALK ABOUT THE--
I'M FINE. I'M GREAT.
I'D STILL LIKE TO DO A FULL PHYSICAL. YOU'VE BEEN THROUGH...
GO GET SOME PIZZA. SHIRLEY'S OR GRILLO'S--YOU PICK IT.
CAN WE GET THE MEAT LOVERS'?!
NO HAMBURGER!
YOU TWO FIGHT IT OUT. JUST GO OUT BACK, OKAY? I'M HUNGRY AND I DON'T WANT ALL THOSE JERKS OUTSIDE SLOWING YOU DOWN.

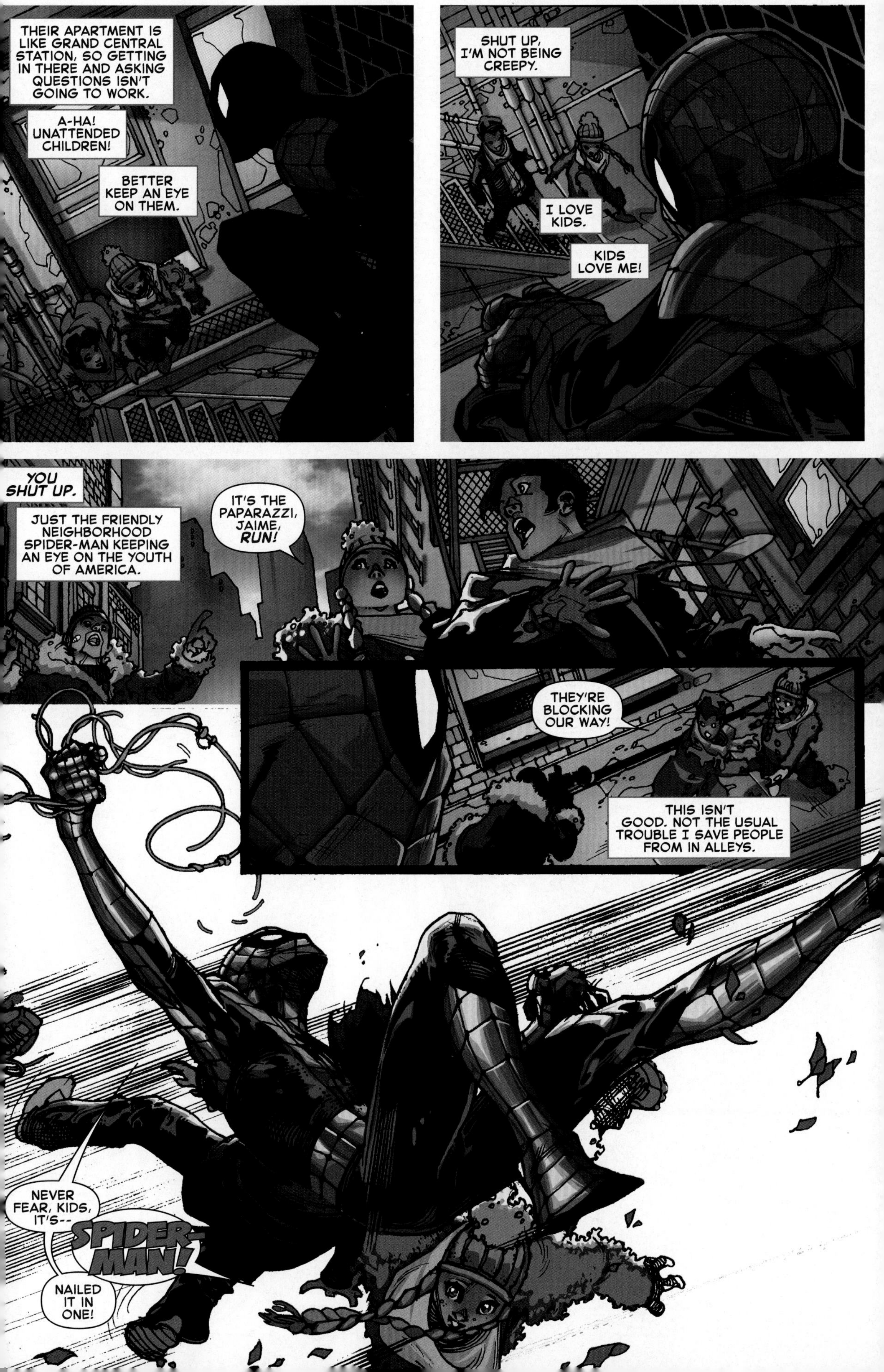

THEIR APARTMENT IS LIKE GRAND CENTRAL STATION, SO GETTING IN THERE AND ASKING QUESTIONS ISN'T GOING TO WORK.
A-HA! UNATTENDED CHILDREN!
BETTER KEEP AN EYE ON THEM.
SHUT UP, I'M NOT BEING CREEPY.
I LOVE KIDS.
KIDS LOVE ME!
YOU SHUT UP.
JUST THE FRIENDLY NEIGHBORHOOD SPIDER-MAN KEEPING AN EYE ON THE YOUTH OF AMERICA.
IT'S THE PAPARAZZI, JAIME, RUN!
THEY'RE BLOCKING OUR WAY!
THIS ISN'T GOOD. NOT THE USUAL TROUBLE I SAVE PEOPLE FROM IN ALLEYS.
NEVER FEAR, KIDS, IT'S--
SPIDER-MAN!
NAILED IT IN ONE!

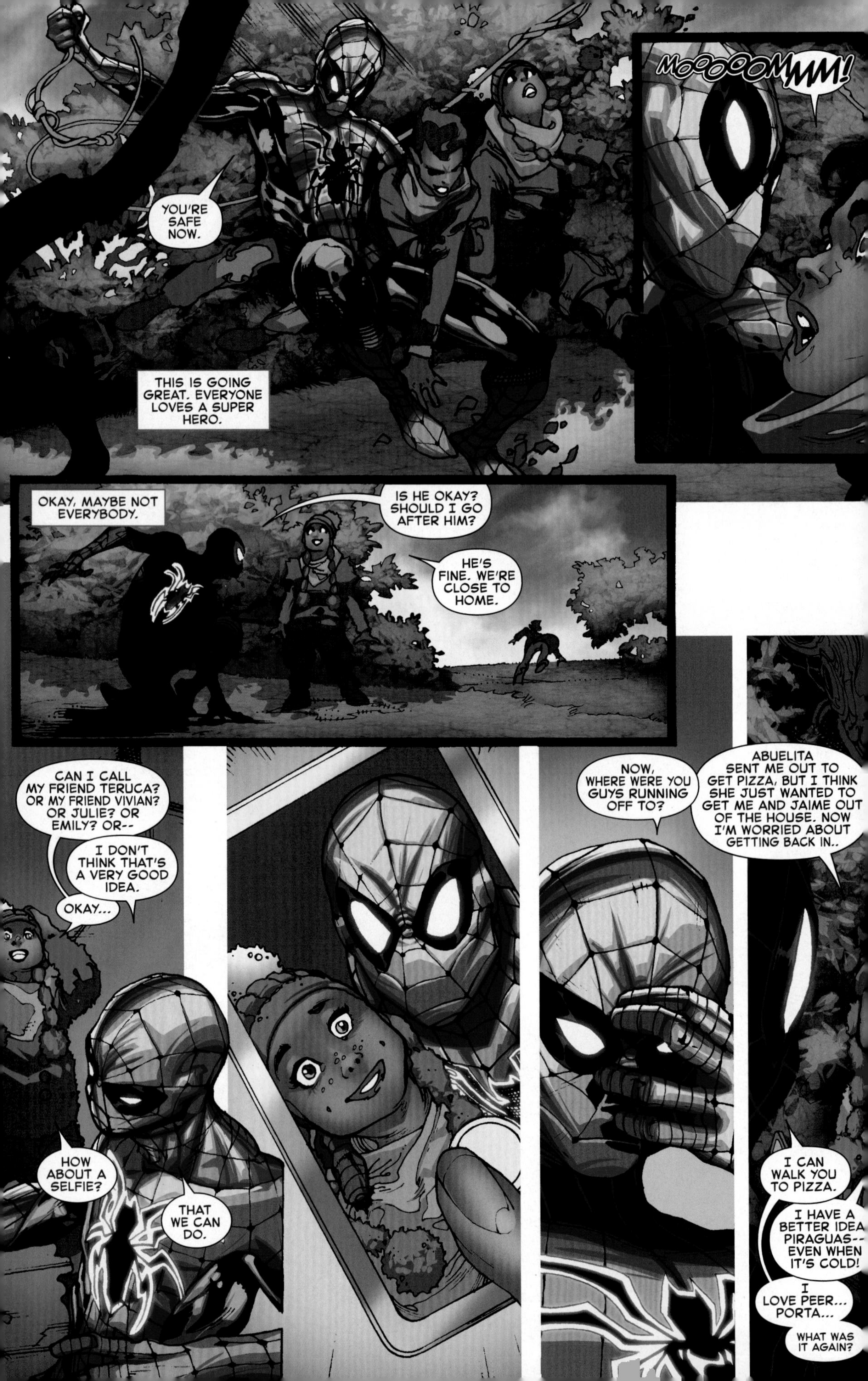
YOU'RE SAFE NOW.
THIS IS GOING GREAT. EVERYONE LOVES A SUPER HERO.
MOOOOOOMMM!
OKAY, MAYBE NOT EVERYBODY.
IS HE OKAY? SHOULD I GO AFTER HIM?
HE'S FINE. WE'RE CLOSE TO HOME.
CAN I CALL MY FRIEND TERUCA? OR MY FRIEND VIVIAN? OR JULIE? OR EMILY? OR--
I DON'T THINK THAT'S A VERY GOOD IDEA.
OKAY...
HOW ABOUT A SELFIE?
THAT WE CAN DO.
NOW, WHERE WERE YOU GUYS RUNNING OFF TO?
ABUELITA SENT ME OUT TO GET PIZZA, BUT I THINK SHE JUST WANTED TO GET ME AND JAIME OUT OF THE HOUSE. NOW I'M WORRIED ABOUT GETTING BACK IN..
I CAN WALK YOU TO PIZZA.
I HAVE A BETTER IDEA PIRAGUAS--EVEN WHEN IT'S COLD!
I LOVE PEER... PORTA...
WHAT WAS IT AGAIN?

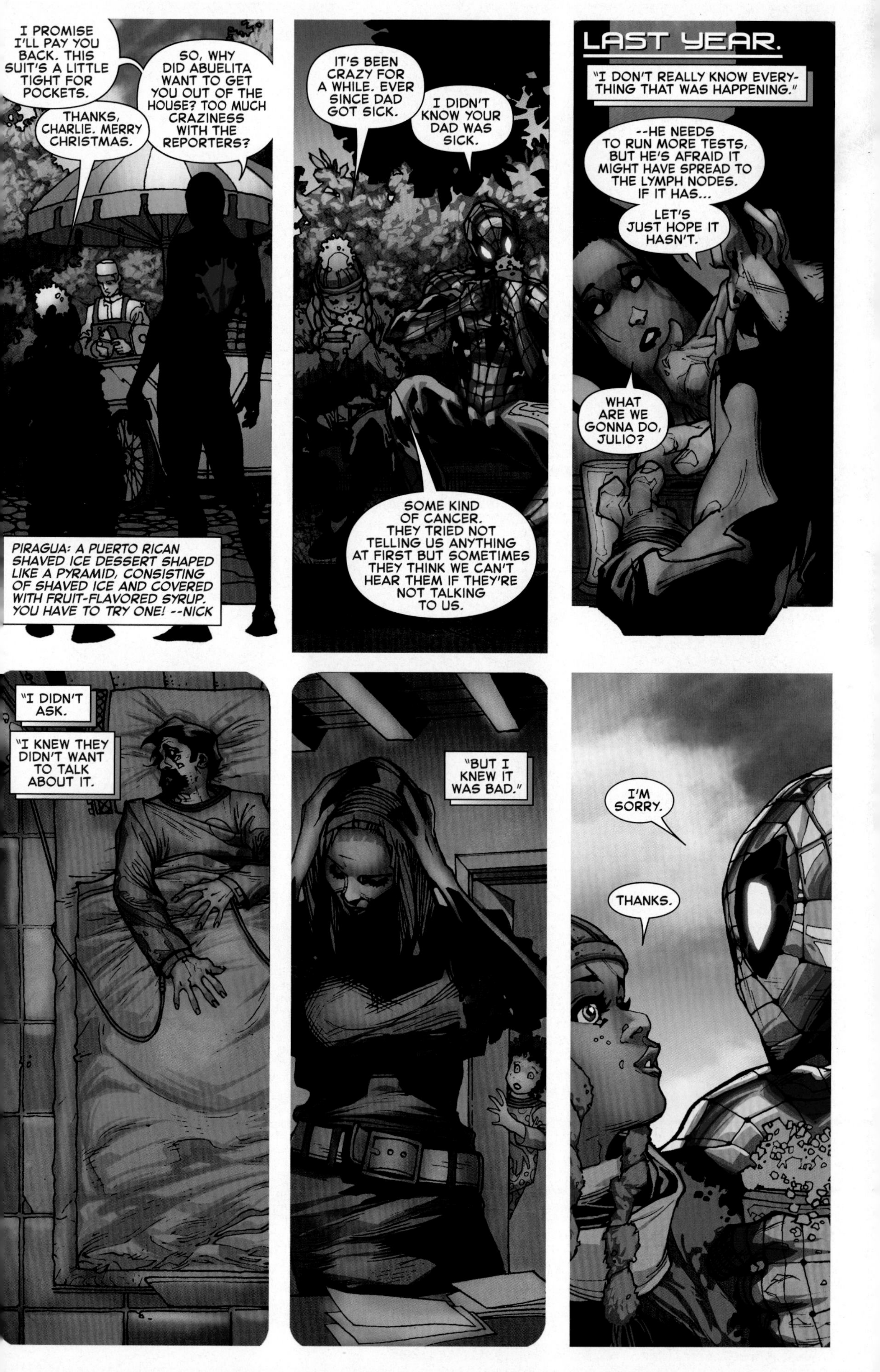
I PROMISE I'LL PAY YOU BACK. THIS SUIT'S A LITTLE TIGHT FOR POCKETS.
THANKS, CHARLIE. MERRY CHRISTMAS.
SO, WHY DID ABUELITA WANT TO GET YOU OUT OF THE HOUSE? TOO MUCH CRAZINESS WITH THE REPORTERS?
PIRAGUA: A PUERTO RICAN SHAVED ICE DESSERT SHAPED LIKE A PYRAMID, CONSISTING OF SHAVED ICE AND COVERED WITH FRUIT-FLAVORED SYRUP. YOU HAVE TO TRY ONE! --NICK
IT'S BEEN CRAZY FOR A WHILE. EVER SINCE DAD GOT SICK.
I DIDN'T KNOW YOUR DAD WAS SICK.
SOME KIND OF CANCER. THEY TRIED NOT TELLING US ANYTHING AT FIRST BUT SOMETIMES THEY THINK WE CAN'T HEAR THEM IF THEY'RE NOT TALKING TO US.
LAST YEAR.
"I DON'T REALLY KNOW EVERYTHING THAT WAS HAPPENING."
--HE NEEDS TO RUN MORE TESTS, BUT HE'S AFRAID IT MIGHT HAVE SPREAD TO THE LYMPH NODES. IF IT HAS...
LET'S JUST HOPE IT HASN'T.
WHAT ARE WE GONNA DO, JULIO?
"I DIDN'T ASK.
"I KNEW THEY DIDN'T WANT TO TALK ABOUT IT.
"BUT I KNEW IT WAS BAD."
I'M SORRY.
THANKS.

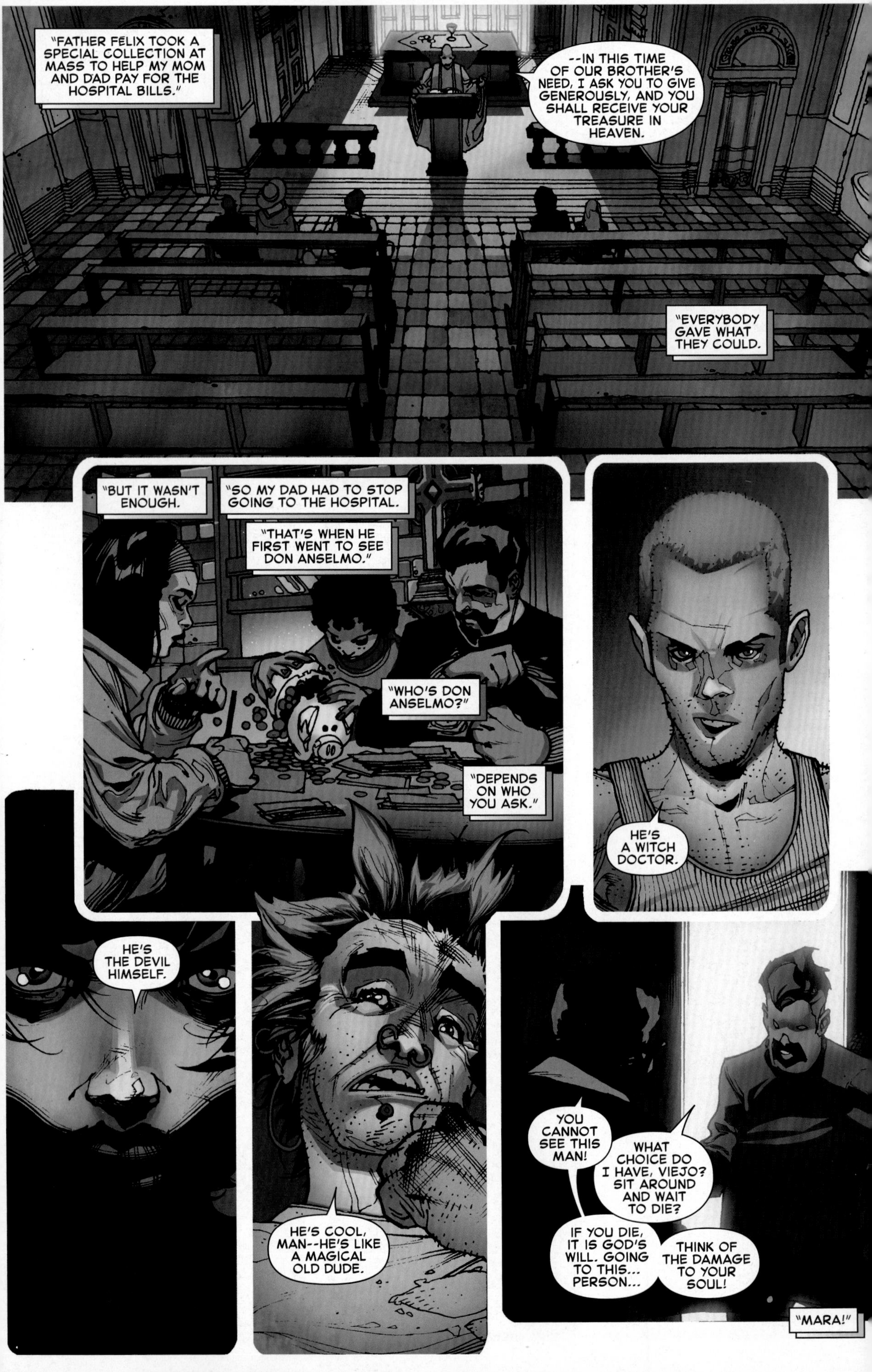
"FATHER FELIX TOOK A SPECIAL COLLECTION AT MASS TO HELP MY MOM AND DAD PAY FOR THE HOSPITAL BILLS."
--IN THIS TIME OF OUR BROTHER'S NEED, I ASK YOU TO GIVE GENEROUSLY, AND YOU SHALL RECEIVE YOUR TREASURE IN HEAVEN.
"EVERYBODY GAVE WHAT THEY COULD.
"BUT IT WASN'T ENOUGH.
"SO MY DAD HAD TO STOP GOING TO THE HOSPITAL.
"THAT'S WHEN HE FIRST WENT TO SEE DON ANSELMO."
"WHO'S DON ANSELMO?"
"DEPENDS ON WHO YOU ASK."
HE'S A WITCH DOCTOR.
HE'S THE DEVIL HIMSELF.
HE'S COOL, MAN--HE'S LIKE A MAGICAL OLD DUDE.
YOU CANNOT SEE THIS MAN!
WHAT CHOICE DO I HAVE, VIEJO? SIT AROUND AND WAIT TO DIE?
IF YOU DIE, IT IS GOD'S WILL. GOING TO THIS... PERSON...
THINK OF THE DAMAGE TO YOUR SOUL!
"MARA!"

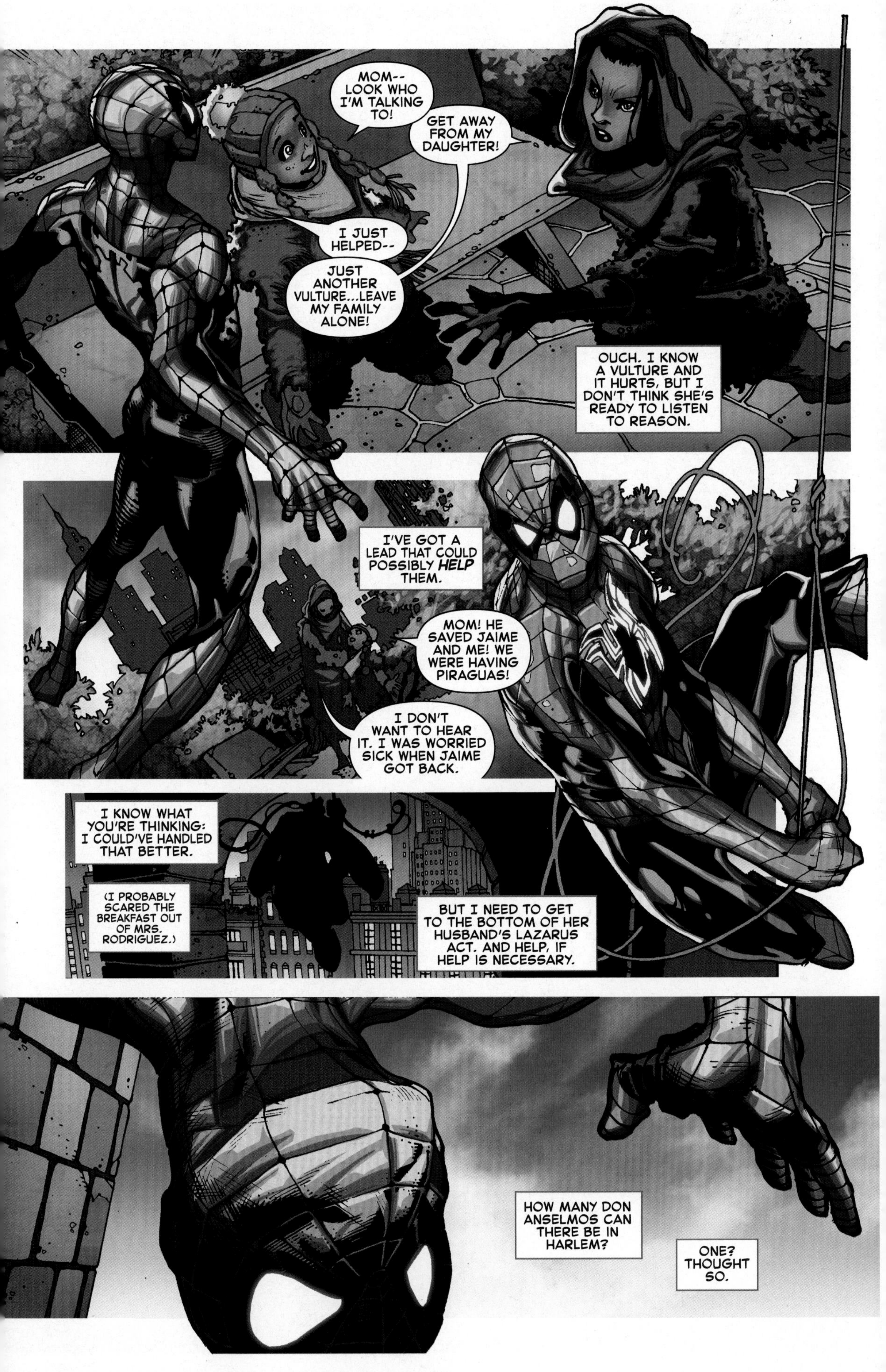
MOM-- LOOK WHO I'M TALKING TO!
GET AWAY FROM MY DAUGHTER!
I JUST HELPED--
JUST ANOTHER VULTURE...LEAVE MY FAMILY ALONE!
OUCH. I KNOW A VULTURE AND IT HURTS, BUT I DON'T THINK SHE'S READY TO LISTEN TO REASON.
I'VE GOT A LEAD THAT COULD POSSIBLY HELP THEM.
MOM! HE SAVED JAIME AND ME! WE WERE HAVING PIRAGUAS!
I DON'T WANT TO HEAR IT. I WAS WORRIED SICK WHEN JAIME GOT BACK.
I KNOW WHAT YOU'RE THINKING: I COULD'VE HANDLED THAT BETTER.
(I PROBABLY SCARED THE BREAKFAST OUT OF MRS. RODRIGUEZ.)
BUT I NEED TO GET TO THE BOTTOM OF HER HUSBAND'S LAZARUS ACT. AND HELP, IF HELP IS NECESSARY.
HOW MANY DON ANSELMOS CAN THERE BE IN HARLEM?
ONE? THOUGHT SO.

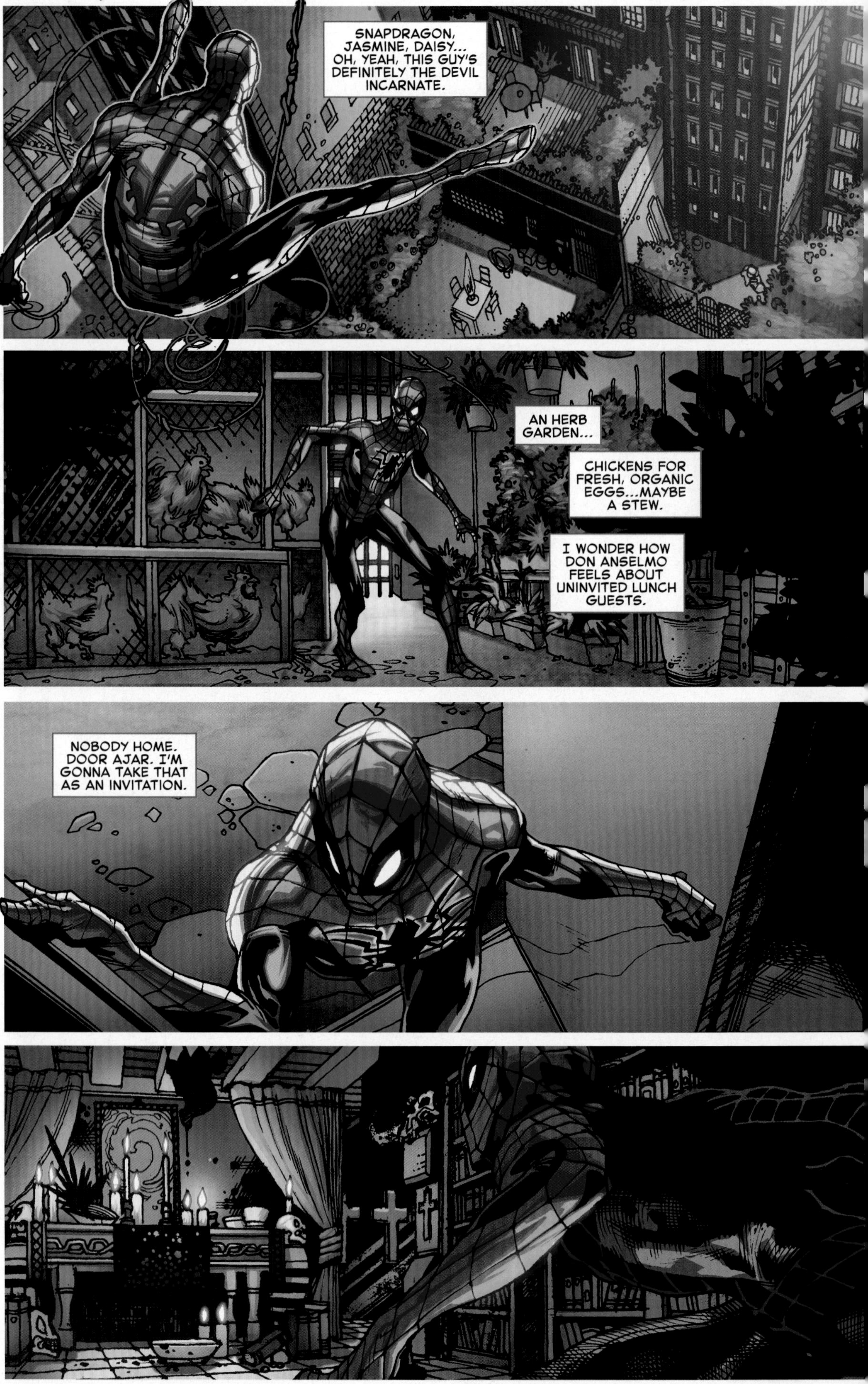
SNAPDRAGON, JASMINE, DAISY... OH, YEAH, THIS GUY'S DEFINITELY THE DEVIL INCARNATE.
AN HERB GARDEN...
CHICKENS FOR FRESH, ORGANIC EGGS...MAYBE A STEW.
I WONDER HOW DON ANSELMO FEELS ABOUT UNINVITED LUNCH GUESTS.
NOBODY HOME. DOOR AJAR. I'M GONNA TAKE THAT AS AN INVITATION.

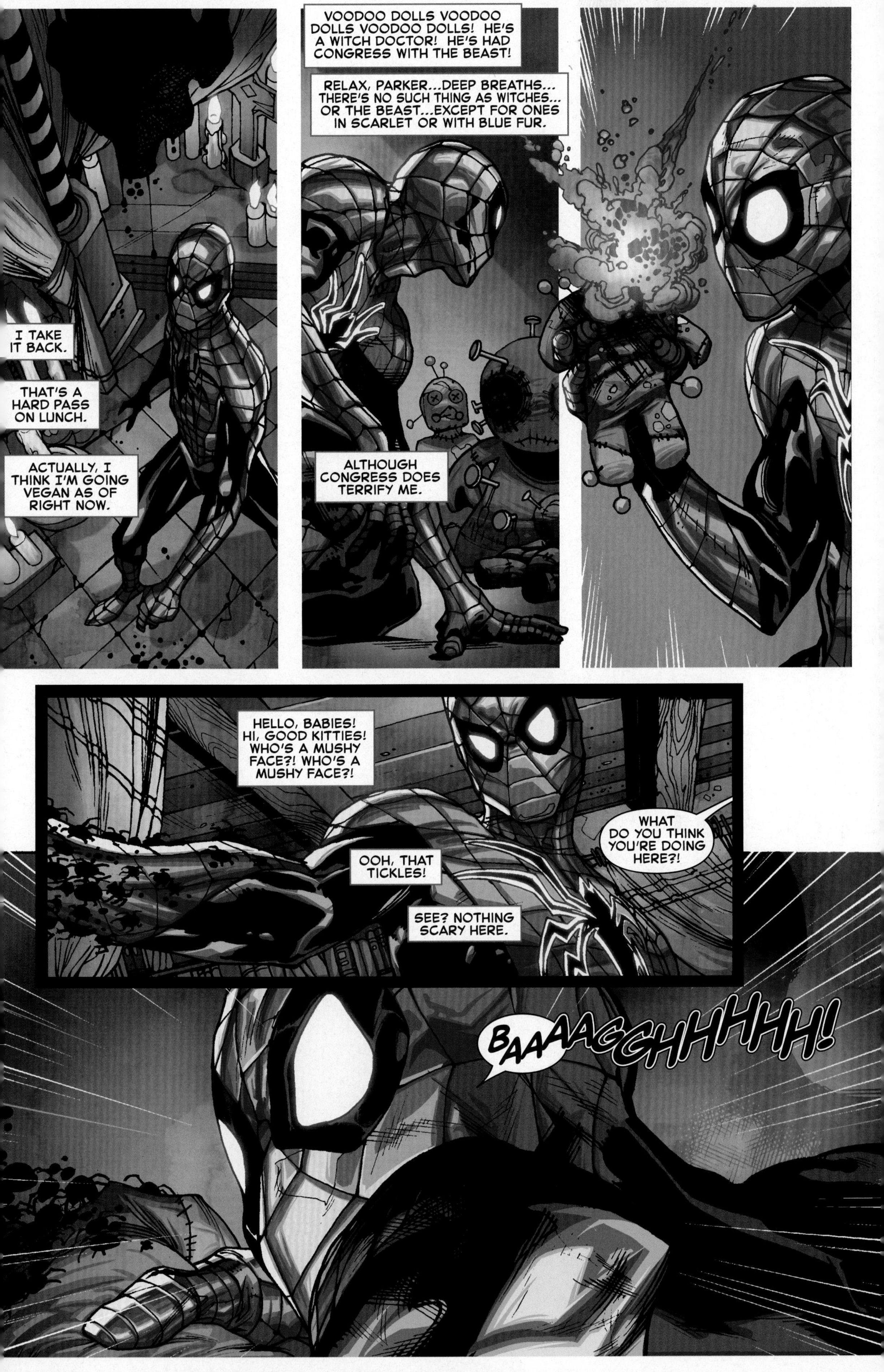
I TAKE IT BACK.
THAT'S A HARD PASS ON LUNCH.
ACTUALLY, I THINK I'M GOING VEGAN AS OF RIGHT NOW.
VOODOO DOLLS VOODOO DOLLS VOODOO DOLLS! HE'S A WITCH DOCTOR! HE'S HAD CONGRESS WITH THE BEAST!
RELAX, PARKER...DEEP BREATHS... THERE'S NO SUCH THING AS WITCHES... OR THE BEAST...EXCEPT FOR ONES IN SCARLET OR WITH BLUE FUR.
ALTHOUGH CONGRESS DOES TERRIFY ME.
HELLO, BABIES! HI, GOOD KITTIES! WHO'S A MUSHY FACE?! WHO'S A MUSHY FACE?!
OOH, THAT TICKLES!
SEE? NOTHING SCARY HERE.
WHAT DO YOU THINK YOU'RE DOING HERE?!
BAAAAGGHHHHHH!

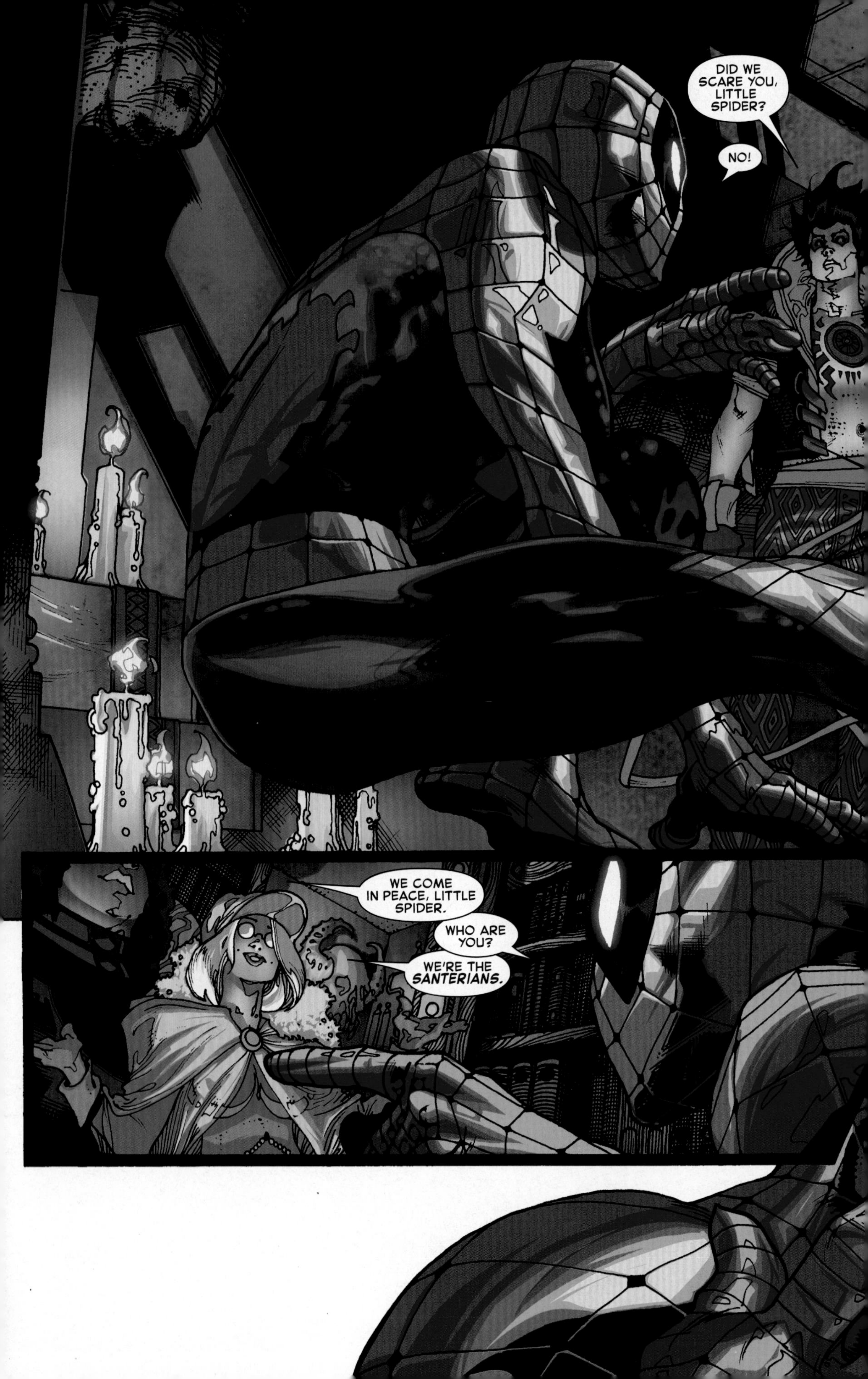
DID WE SCARE YOU, LITTLE SPIDER?
NO!
WE COME IN PEACE, LITTLE SPIDER.
WHO ARE YOU?
WE'RE THE SANTERIANS.

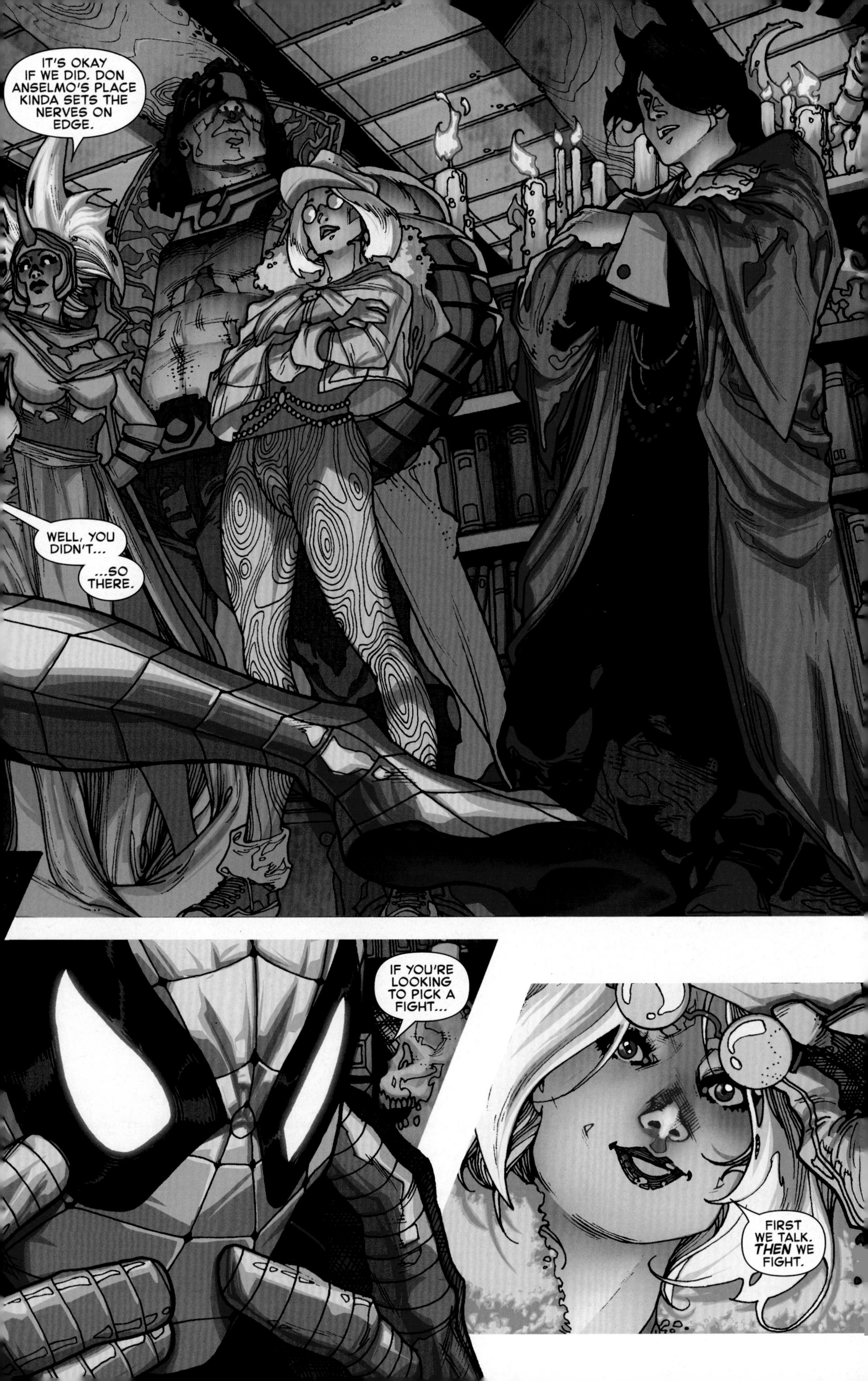
IT'S OKAY IF WE DID. DON ANSELMO'S PLACE KINDA SETS THE NERVES ON EDGE.
WELL, YOU DIDN'T...
...SO THERE.
IF YOU'RE LOOKING TO PICK A FIGHT...
FIRST WE TALK. *THEN* WE FIGHT.

1.2

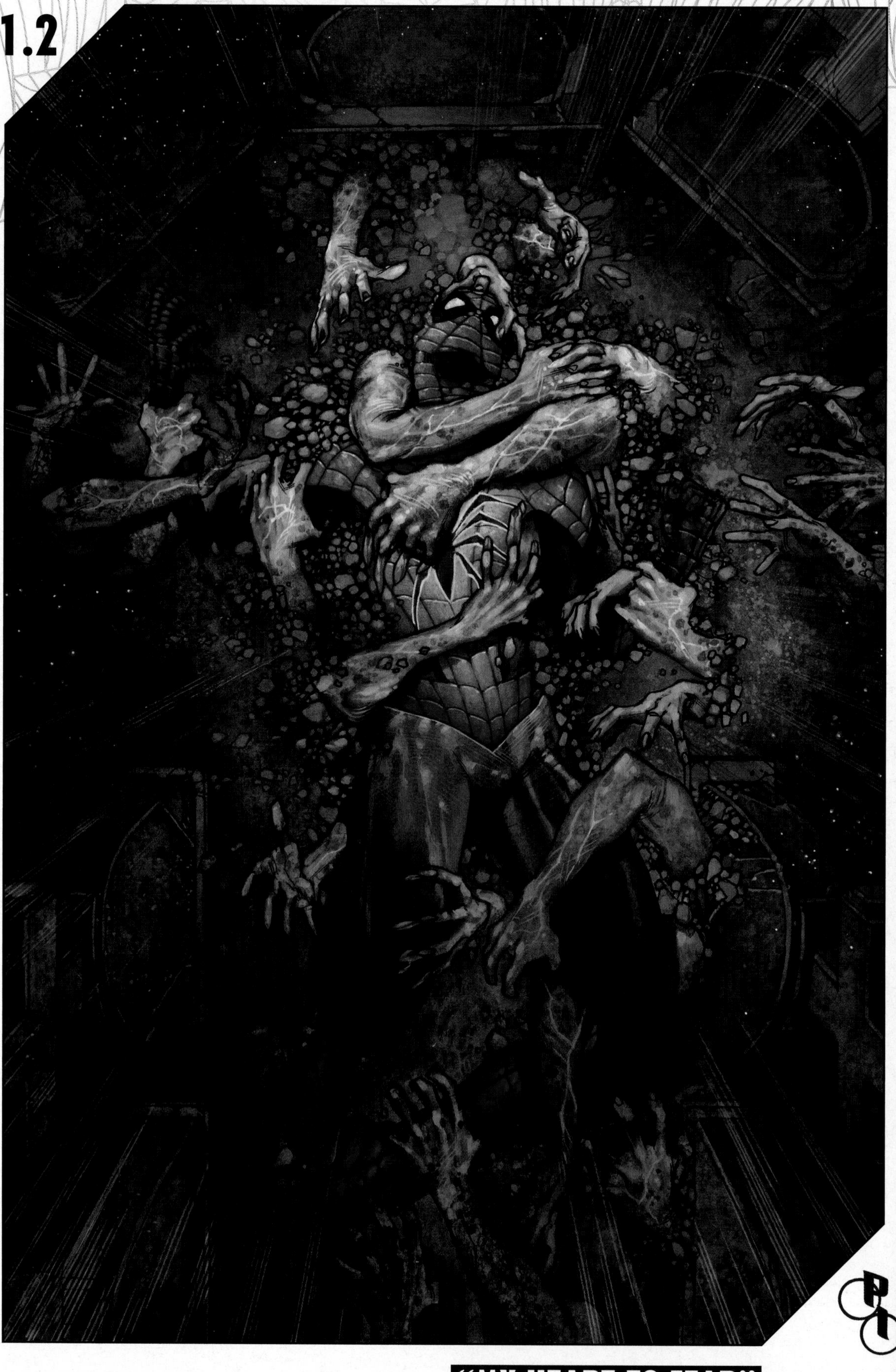

"MY HEART TO FEAR"

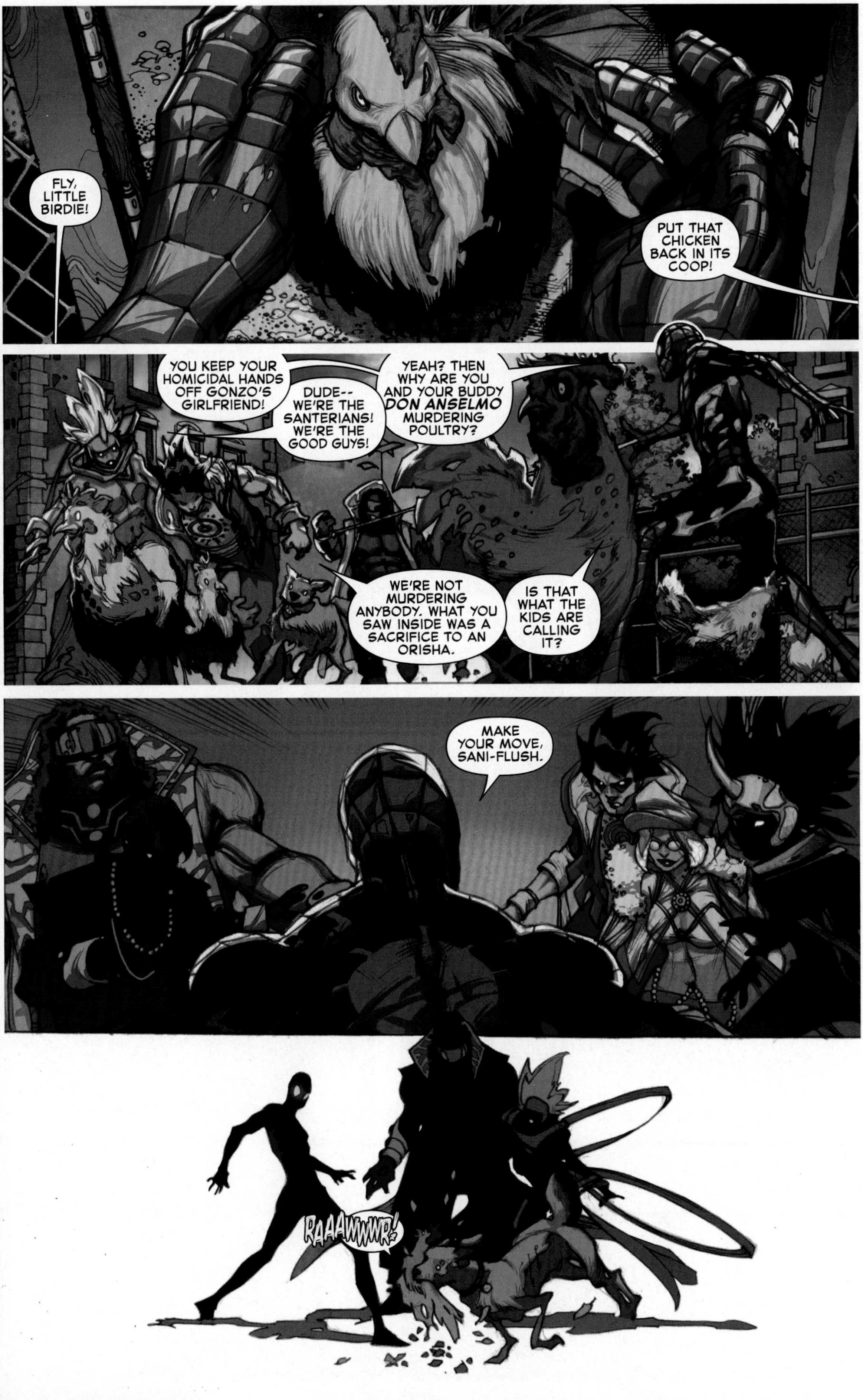
FLY, LITTLE BIRDIE!
PUT THAT CHICKEN BACK IN ITS COOP!
YOU KEEP YOUR HOMICIDAL HANDS OFF GONZO'S GIRLFRIEND!
DUDE-- WE'RE THE SANTERIANS! WE'RE THE GOOD GUYS!
YEAH? THEN WHY ARE YOU AND YOUR BUDDY DON ANSELMO MURDERING POULTRY?
WE'RE NOT MURDERING ANYBODY. WHAT YOU SAW INSIDE WAS A SACRIFICE TO AN ORISHA.
IS THAT WHAT THE KIDS ARE CALLING IT?
MAKE YOUR MOVE, SANI-FLUSH.
RAAAWWWR!

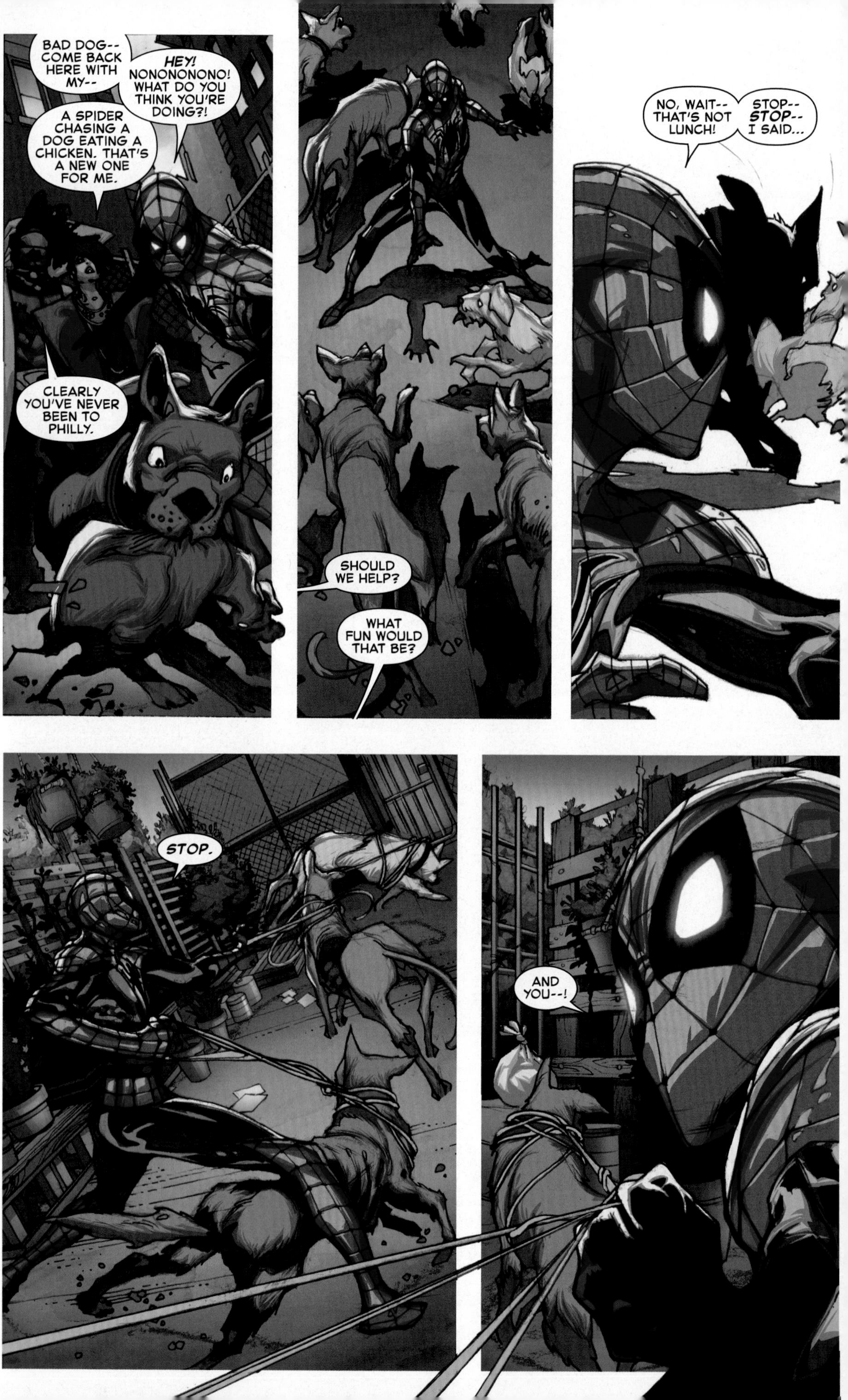
BAD DOG-- COME BACK HERE WITH MY--
HEY! NONONONONO! WHAT DO YOU THINK YOU'RE DOING?!
A SPIDER CHASING A DOG EATING A CHICKEN. THAT'S A NEW ONE FOR ME.
CLEARLY YOU'VE NEVER BEEN TO PHILLY.
SHOULD WE HELP?
WHAT FUN WOULD THAT BE?
NO, WAIT-- THAT'S NOT LUNCH!
STOP-- STOP-- I SAID...
STOP.
AND YOU--!

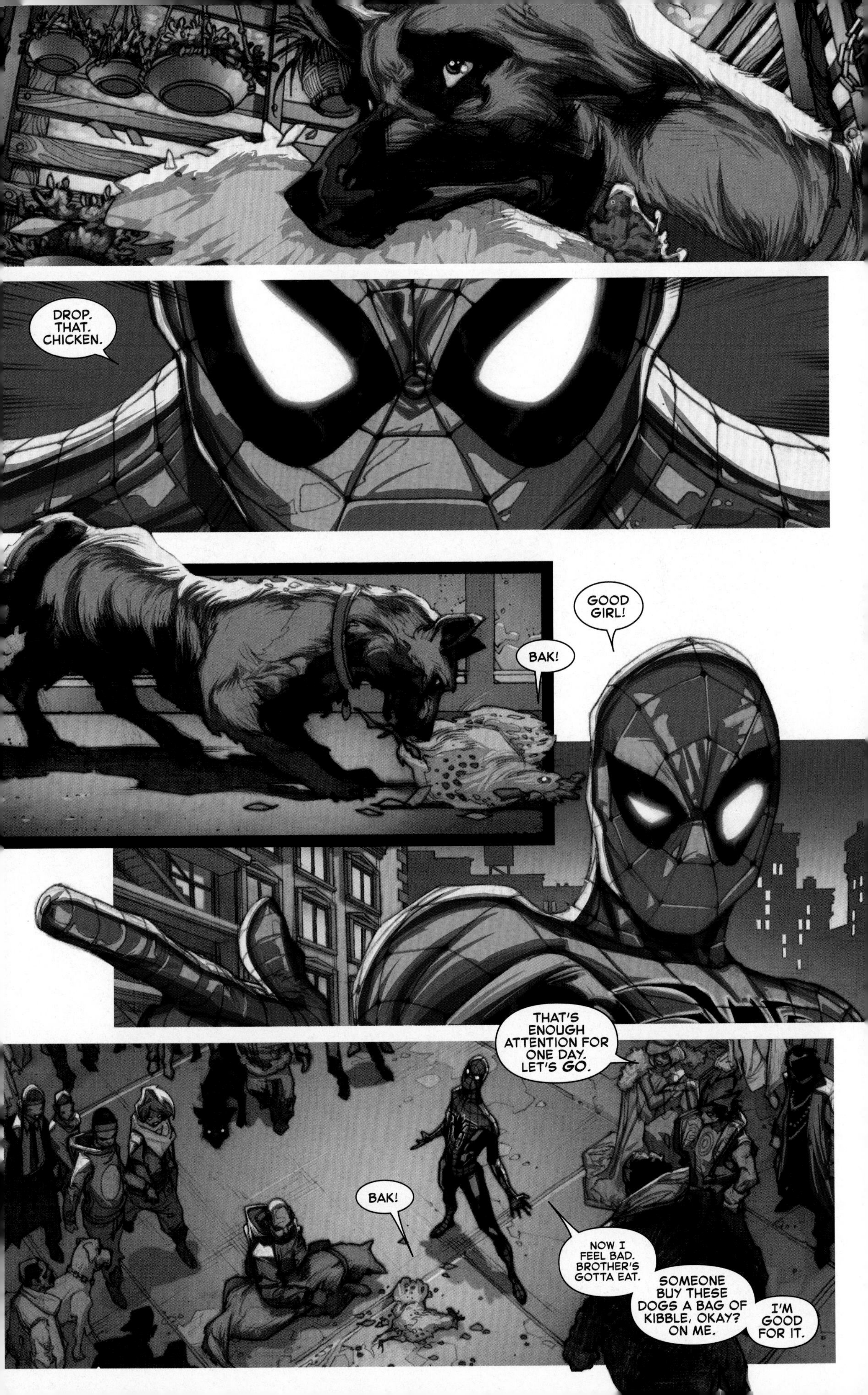
DROP. THAT. CHICKEN.
BAK!
GOOD GIRL!
THAT'S ENOUGH ATTENTION FOR ONE DAY. LET'S GO.
BAK!
NOW I FEEL BAD. BROTHER'S GOTTA EAT.
SOMEONE BUY THESE DOGS A BAG OF KIBBLE, OKAY? ON ME.
I'M GOOD FOR IT.

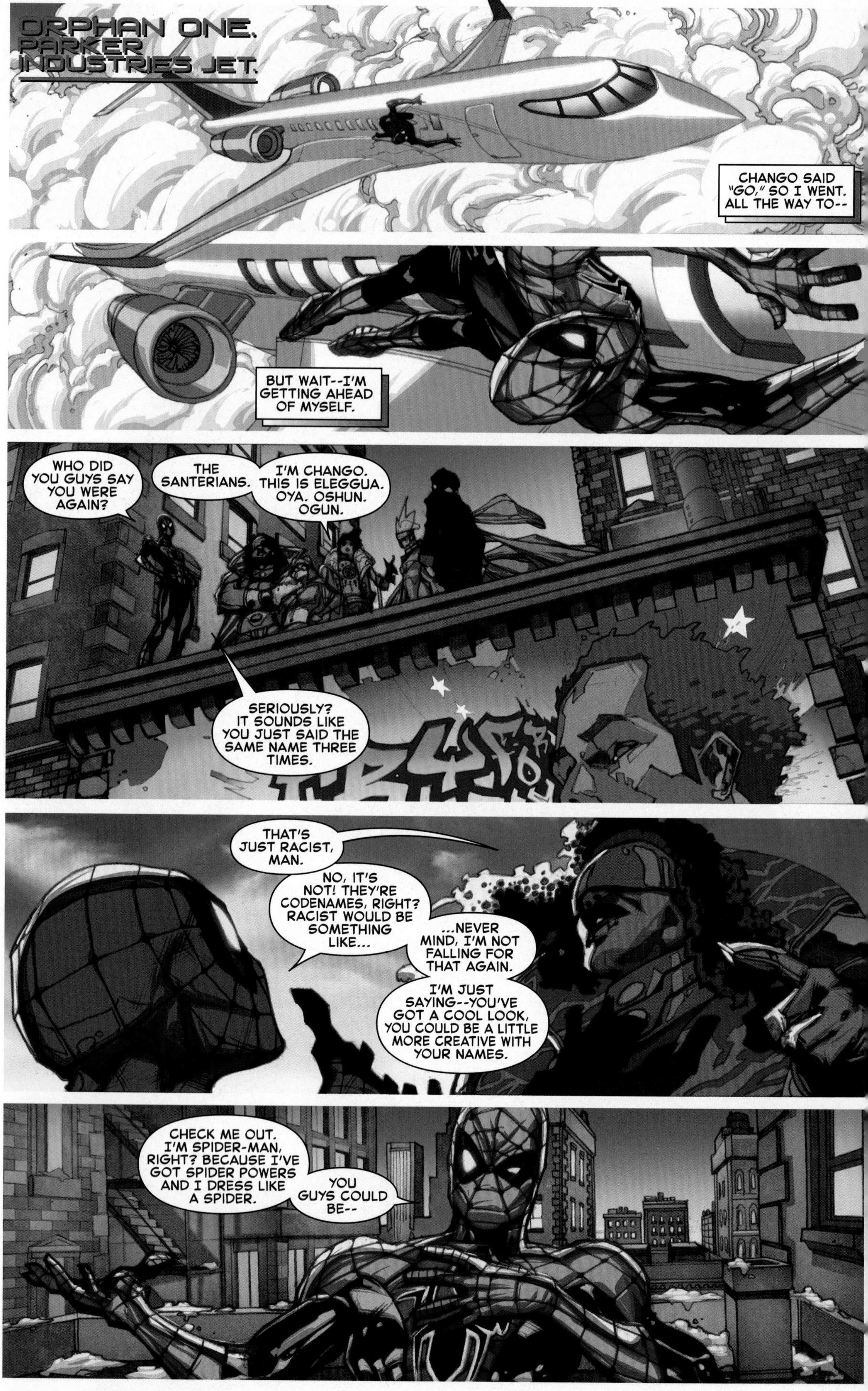
ORPHAN ONE.
PARKER INDUSTRIES JET.
CHANGO SAID "GO," SO I WENT. ALL THE WAY TO--
BUT WAIT--I'M GETTING AHEAD OF MYSELF.
WHO DID YOU GUYS SAY YOU WERE AGAIN?
THE SANTERIANS.
I'M CHANGO. THIS IS ELEGGUA. OYA. OSHUN. OGUN.
SERIOUSLY? IT SOUNDS LIKE YOU JUST SAID THE SAME NAME THREE TIMES.
THAT'S JUST RACIST, MAN.
NO, IT'S NOT! THEY'RE CODENAMES, RIGHT? RACIST WOULD BE SOMETHING LIKE...
...NEVER MIND, I'M NOT FALLING FOR THAT AGAIN.
I'M JUST SAYING--YOU'VE GOT A COOL LOOK, YOU COULD BE A LITTLE MORE CREATIVE WITH YOUR NAMES.
CHECK ME OUT. I'M SPIDER-MAN, RIGHT? BECAUSE I'VE GOT SPIDER POWERS AND I DRESS LIKE A SPIDER.
YOU GUYS COULD BE--

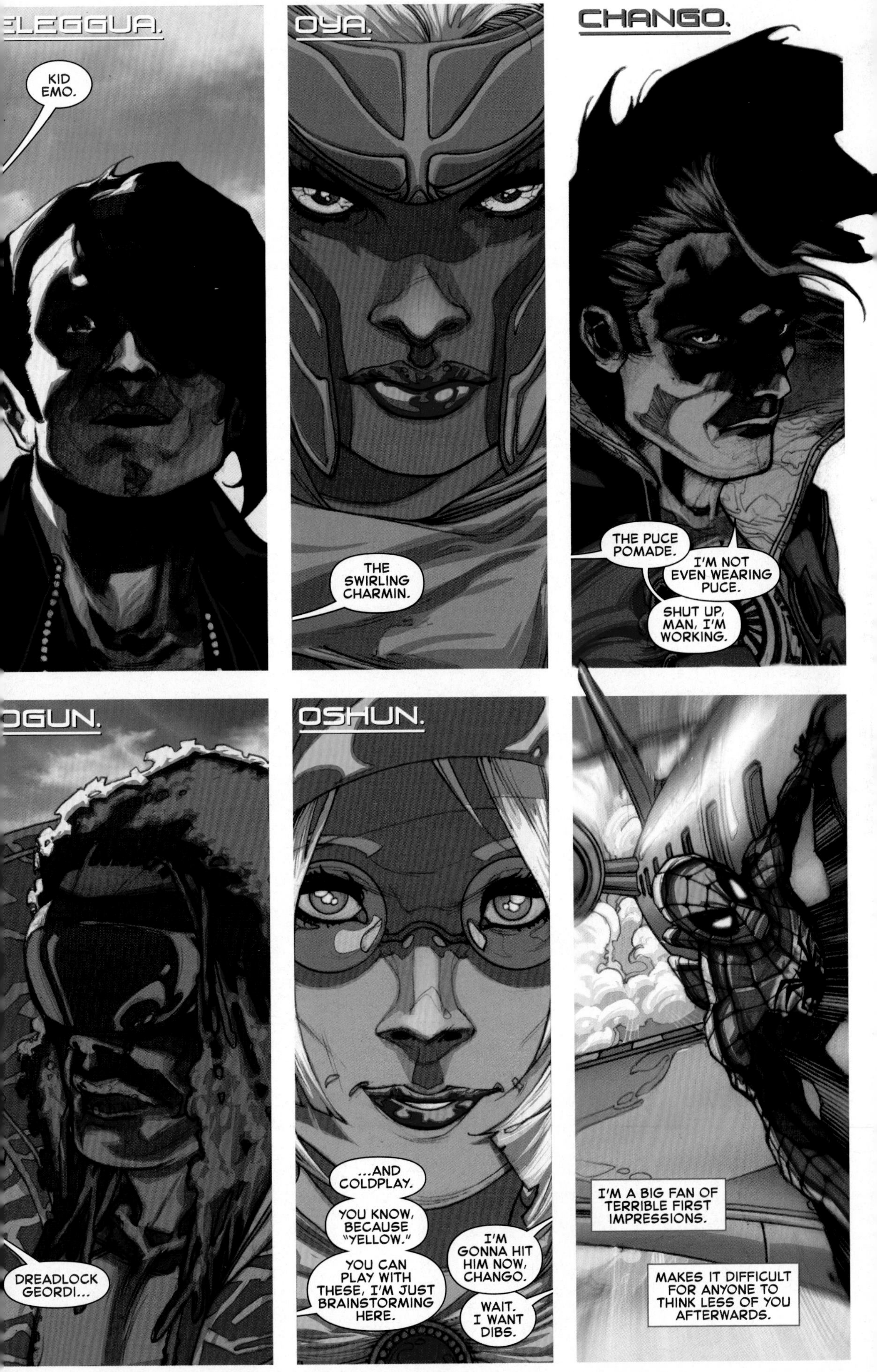

ELEGGUA.
KID EMO.
OYA.
THE SWIRLING CHARMIN.
CHANGO.
THE PUCE POMADE.
I'M NOT EVEN WEARING PUCE.
SHUT UP, MAN, I'M WORKING.
OGUN.
DREADLOCK GEORDI...
OSHUN.
...AND COLDPLAY.
YOU KNOW, BECAUSE "YELLOW."
YOU CAN PLAY WITH THESE, I'M JUST BRAINSTORMING HERE.
I'M GONNA HIT HIM NOW, CHANGO.
WAIT. I WANT DIBS.
I'M A BIG FAN OF TERRIBLE FIRST IMPRESSIONS.
MAKES IT DIFFICULT FOR ANYONE TO THINK LESS OF YOU AFTERWARDS.

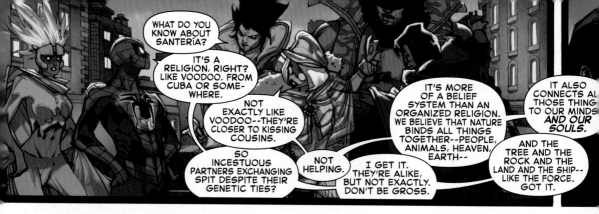

WHAT DO YOU KNOW ABOUT SANTERÍA?

IT'S A RELIGION, RIGHT? LIKE VOODOO. FROM CUBA OR SOME-WHERE.

NOT EXACTLY LIKE VOODOO--THEY'RE CLOSER TO KISSING COUSINS.

SO INCESTUOUS PARTNERS EXCHANGING SPIT DESPITE THEIR GENETIC TIES?

NOT HELPING.

I GET IT. THEY'RE ALIKE, BUT NOT EXACTLY. DON'T BE GROSS.

IT'S MORE OF A BELIEF SYSTEM THAN AN ORGANIZED RELIGION. WE BELIEVE THAT NATURE BINDS ALL THINGS TOGETHER--PEOPLE, ANIMALS, HEAVEN, EARTH--

IT ALSO CONNECTS AL THOSE THING TO OUR MINDS AND OUR SOULS.

AND THE TREE AND THE ROCK AND THE LAND AND THE SHIP-- LIKE THE FORCE. GOT IT.

POWERS. GOT IT.

YOU MAKE IT HUMID. WHAT A GIFT.

I TOLD YOU HE WOULDN'T TAKE US SERIOUSLY.

EASY, HEAT MISER. I'M JOKING. IT'S A THING WITH ME.

AND WHY WOULDN'T I TAKE YOU SERIOUSLY? I'M LISTENING. WE'RE CHATTING. WE'RE BONDING.

FUN'S OVER, FRIEND-O.

POWER DOWN.

THAT'S IT, I'M TORCHING HIM.

CHANGO!

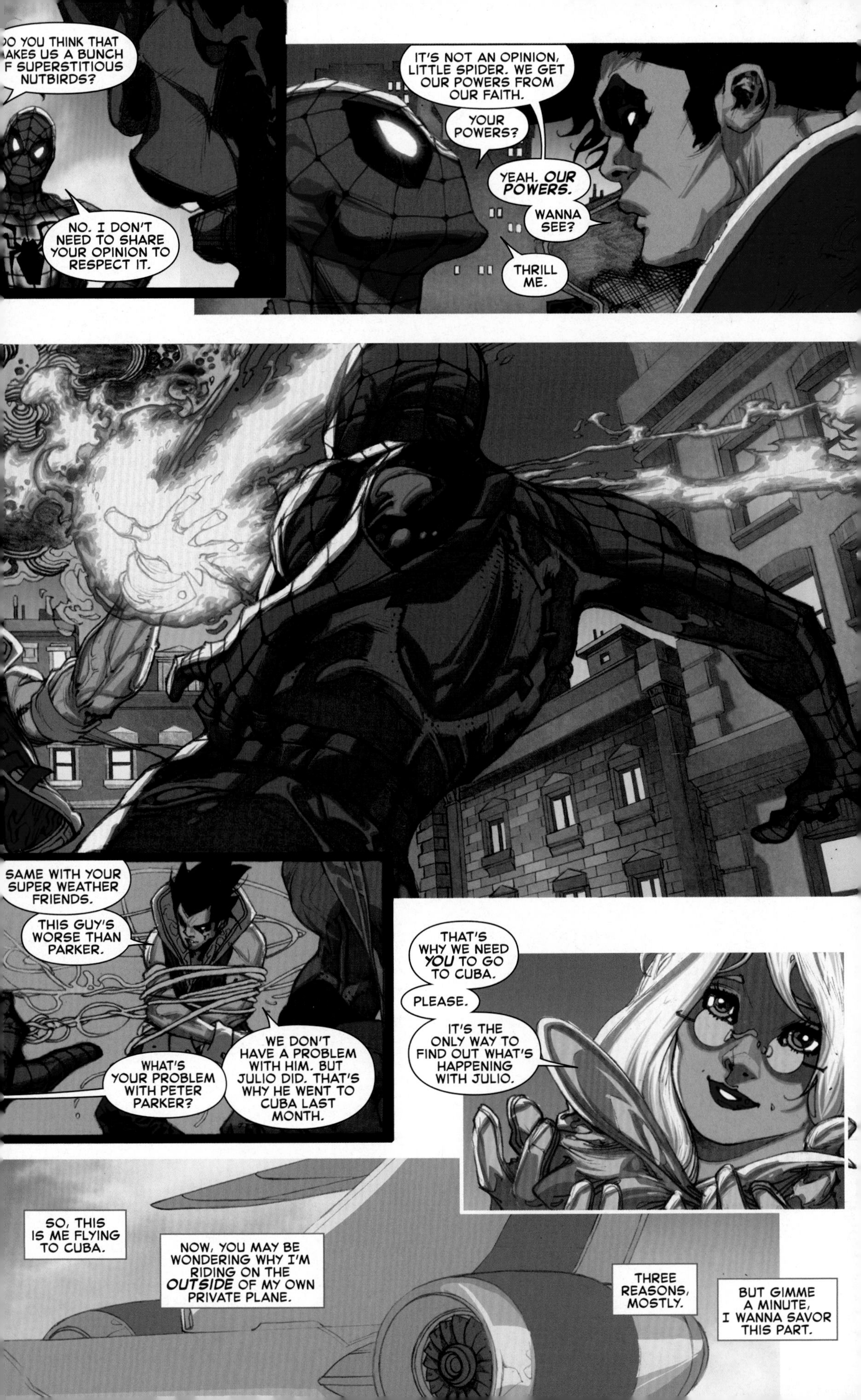

DO YOU THINK THAT MAKES US A BUNCH OF SUPERSTITIOUS NUTBIRDS?
NO. I DON'T NEED TO SHARE YOUR OPINION TO RESPECT IT.
IT'S NOT AN OPINION, LITTLE SPIDER. WE GET OUR POWERS FROM OUR FAITH.
YOUR POWERS?
YEAH. OUR POWERS.
WANNA SEE?
THRILL ME.
SAME WITH YOUR SUPER WEATHER FRIENDS.
THIS GUY'S WORSE THAN PARKER.
WHAT'S YOUR PROBLEM WITH PETER PARKER?
WE DON'T HAVE A PROBLEM WITH HIM. BUT JULIO DID. THAT'S WHY HE WENT TO CUBA LAST MONTH.
THAT'S WHY WE NEED YOU TO GO TO CUBA.
PLEASE.
IT'S THE ONLY WAY TO FIND OUT WHAT'S HAPPENING WITH JULIO.
SO, THIS IS ME FLYING TO CUBA.
NOW, YOU MAY BE WONDERING WHY I'M RIDING ON THE OUTSIDE OF MY OWN PRIVATE PLANE.
THREE REASONS, MOSTLY.
BUT GIMME A MINUTE, I WANNA SAVOR THIS PART.

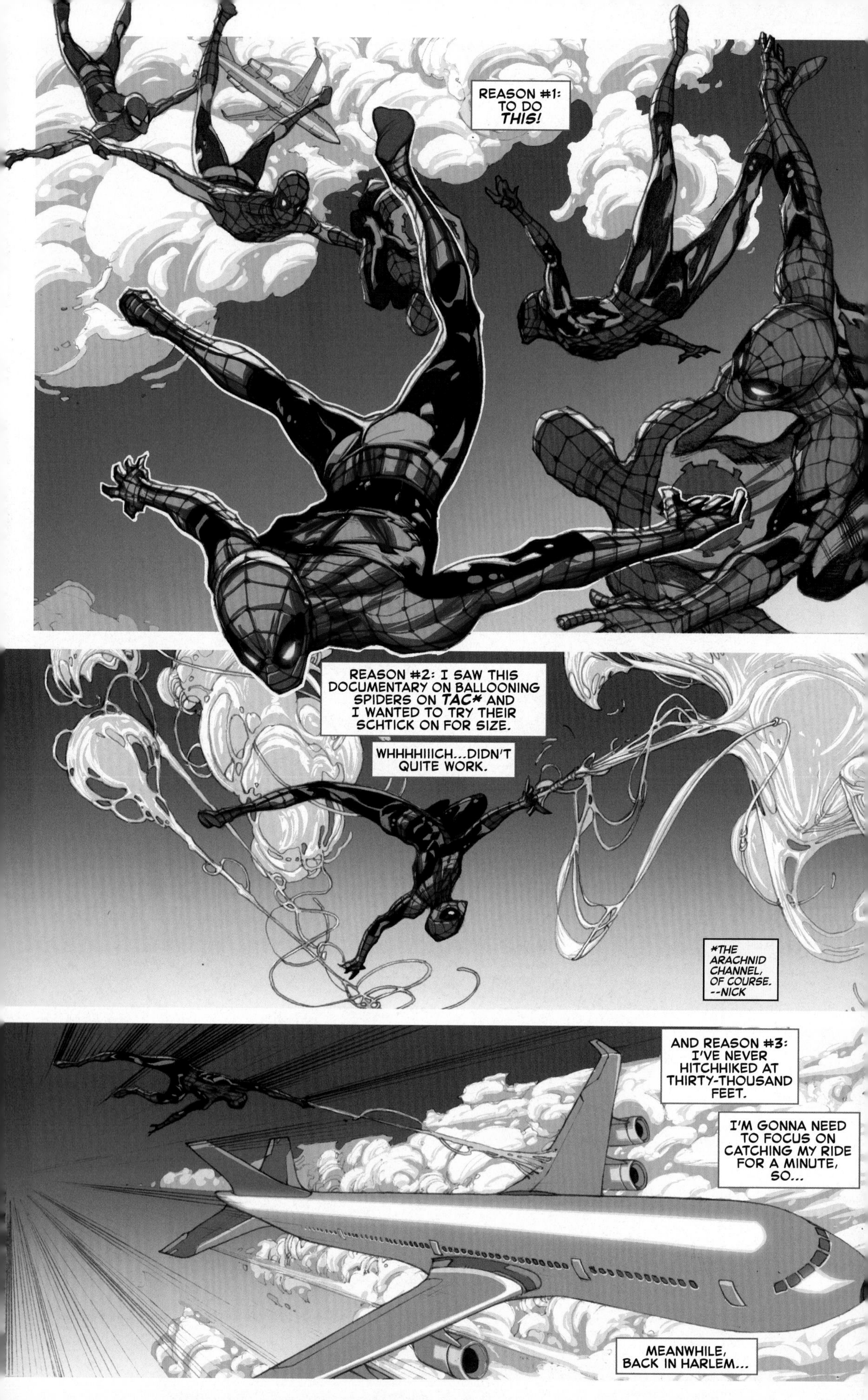
REASON #1: TO DO *THIS!*
REASON #2: I SAW THIS DOCUMENTARY ON BALLOONING SPIDERS ON *TAC** AND I WANTED TO TRY THEIR SCHTICK ON FOR SIZE.
WHHHHIIICH...DIDN'T QUITE WORK.
*THE ARACHNID CHANNEL, OF COURSE. --NICK
AND REASON #3: I'VE NEVER HITCHHIKED AT THIRTY-THOUSAND FEET.
I'M GONNA NEED TO FOCUS ON CATCHING MY RIDE FOR A MINUTE, SO...
MEANWHILE, BACK IN HARLEM...

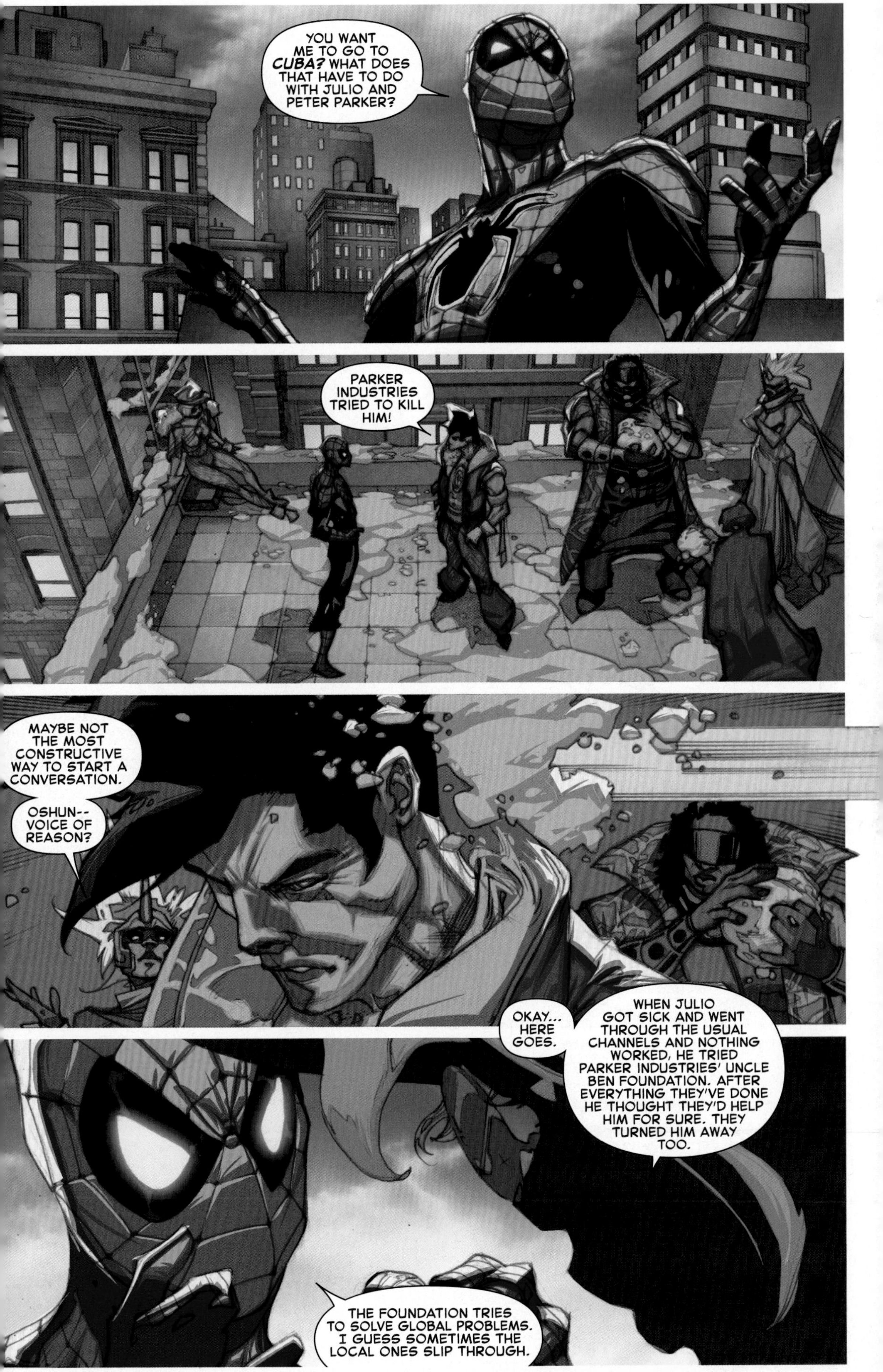
YOU WANT ME TO GO TO CUBA? WHAT DOES THAT HAVE TO DO WITH JULIO AND PETER PARKER?
PARKER INDUSTRIES TRIED TO KILL HIM!
MAYBE NOT THE MOST CONSTRUCTIVE WAY TO START A CONVERSATION.
OSHUN-- VOICE OF REASON?
OKAY... HERE GOES.
WHEN JULIO GOT SICK AND WENT THROUGH THE USUAL CHANNELS AND NOTHING WORKED, HE TRIED PARKER INDUSTRIES' UNCLE BEN FOUNDATION. AFTER EVERYTHING THEY'VE DONE HE THOUGHT THEY'D HELP HIM FOR SURE. THEY TURNED HIM AWAY TOO.
THE FOUNDATION TRIES TO SOLVE GLOBAL PROBLEMS. I GUESS SOMETIMES THE LOCAL ONES SLIP THROUGH.

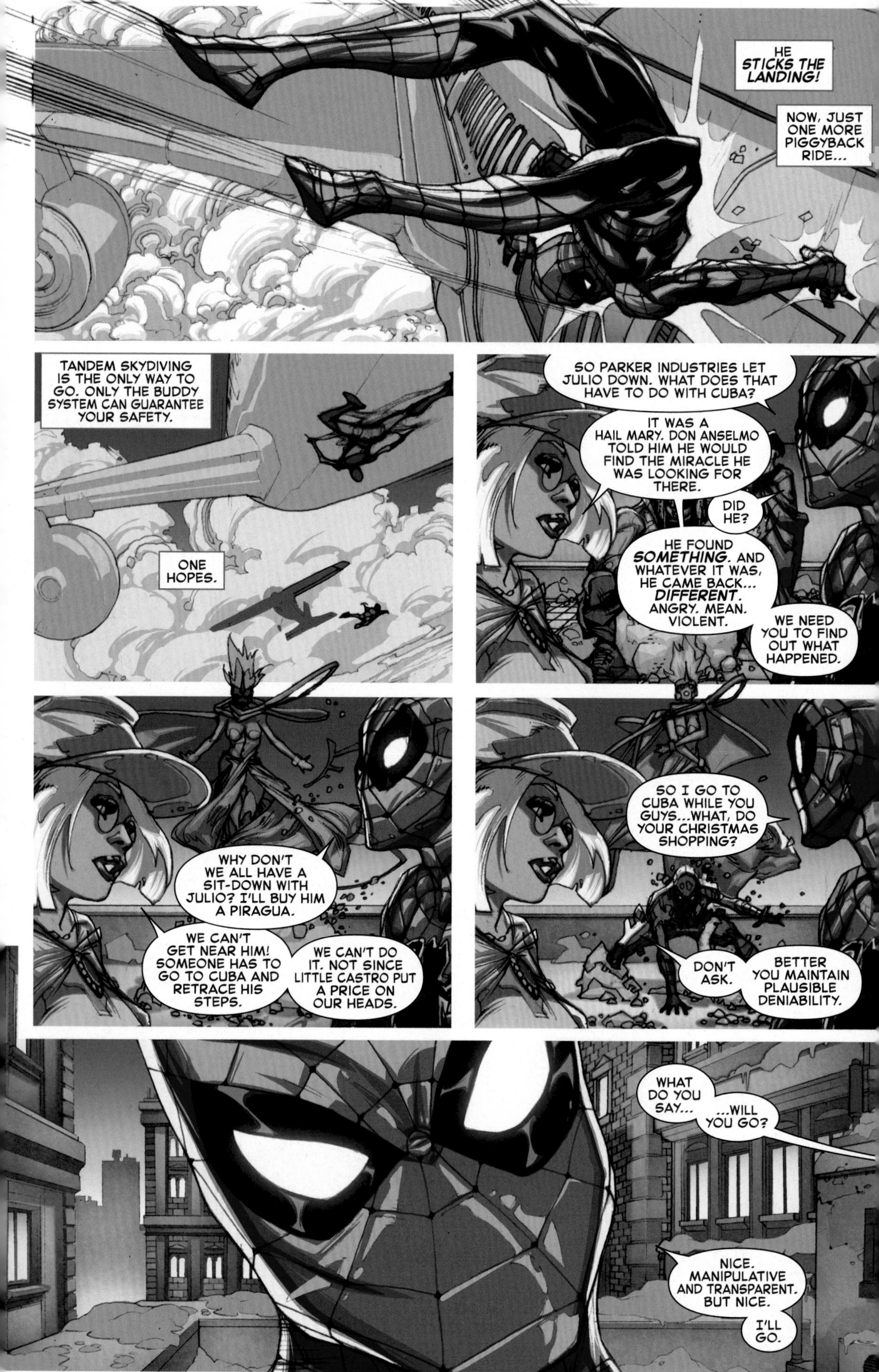
HE *STICKS THE LANDING!*
NOW, JUST ONE MORE PIGGYBACK RIDE...
TANDEM SKYDIVING IS THE ONLY WAY TO GO. ONLY THE BUDDY SYSTEM CAN GUARANTEE YOUR SAFETY.
ONE HOPES.
SO PARKER INDUSTRIES LET JULIO DOWN. WHAT DOES THAT HAVE TO DO WITH CUBA?
IT WAS A HAIL MARY. DON ANSELMO TOLD HIM HE WOULD FIND THE MIRACLE HE WAS LOOKING FOR THERE.
DID HE?
HE FOUND *SOMETHING*. AND WHATEVER IT WAS, HE CAME BACK... *DIFFERENT*. ANGRY. MEAN. VIOLENT.
WE NEED YOU TO FIND OUT WHAT HAPPENED.
WHY DON'T WE ALL HAVE A SIT-DOWN WITH JULIO? I'LL BUY HIM A PIRAGUA.
WE CAN'T GET NEAR HIM! SOMEONE HAS TO GO TO CUBA AND RETRACE HIS STEPS.
WE CAN'T DO IT. NOT SINCE LITTLE CASTRO PUT A PRICE ON OUR HEADS.
SO I GO TO CUBA WHILE YOU GUYS...WHAT, DO YOUR CHRISTMAS SHOPPING?
DON'T ASK.
BETTER YOU MAINTAIN PLAUSIBLE DENIABILITY.
WHAT DO YOU SAY...
...WILL YOU GO?
NICE. MANIPULATIVE AND TRANSPARENT. BUT NICE.
I'LL GO.

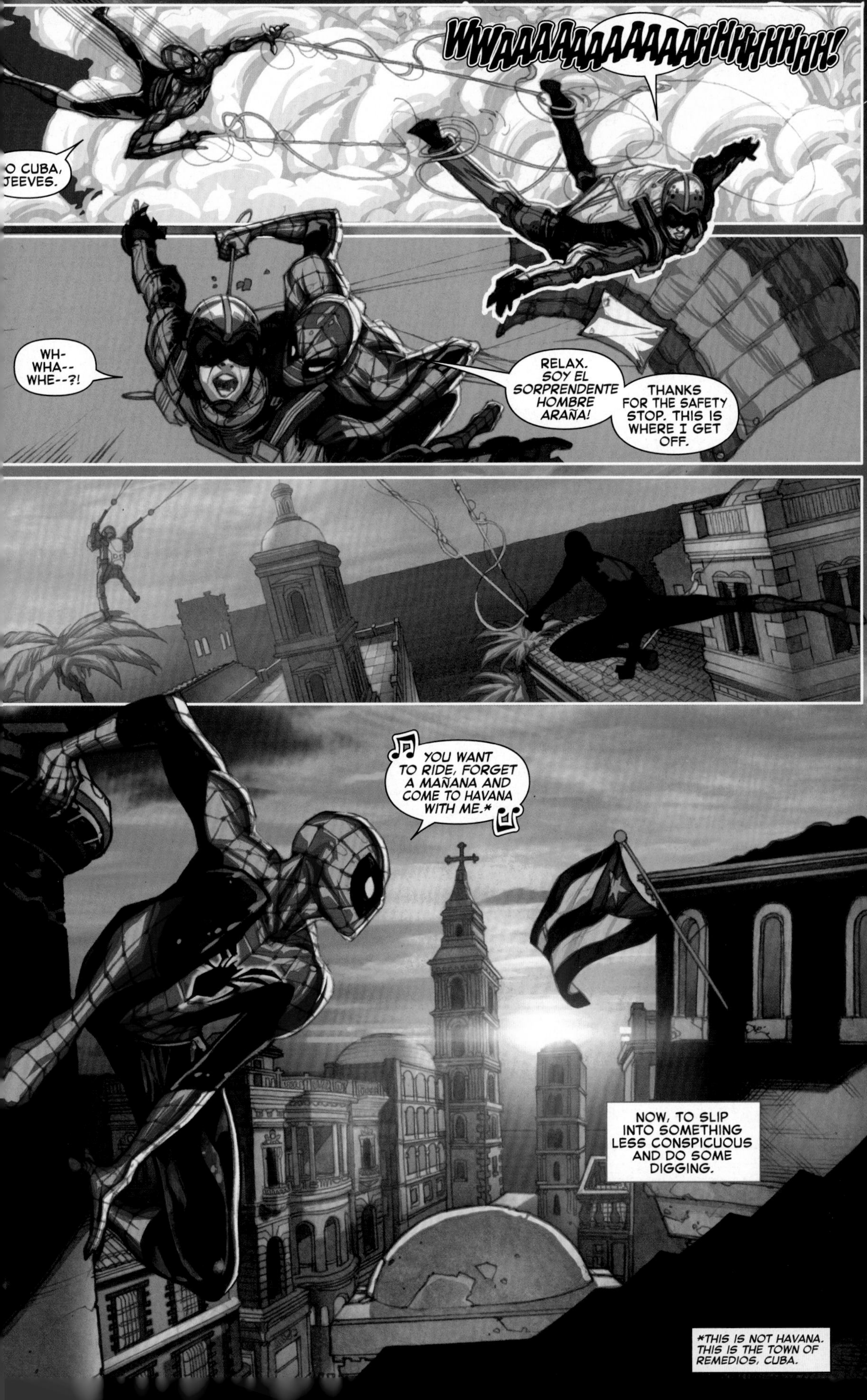

O CUBA, JEEVES.
WWAAAAAAAAAAAAHHHHHHH!
WH- WHA-- WHE--?!
RELAX. SOY EL SORPRENDENTE HOMBRE ARAÑA!
THANKS FOR THE SAFETY STOP. THIS IS WHERE I GET OFF.
YOU WANT TO RIDE, FORGET A MAÑANA AND COME TO HAVANA WITH ME.*
NOW, TO SLIP INTO SOMETHING LESS CONSPICUOUS AND DO SOME DIGGING.
*THIS IS NOT HAVANA. THIS IS THE TOWN OF REMEDIOS, CUBA.

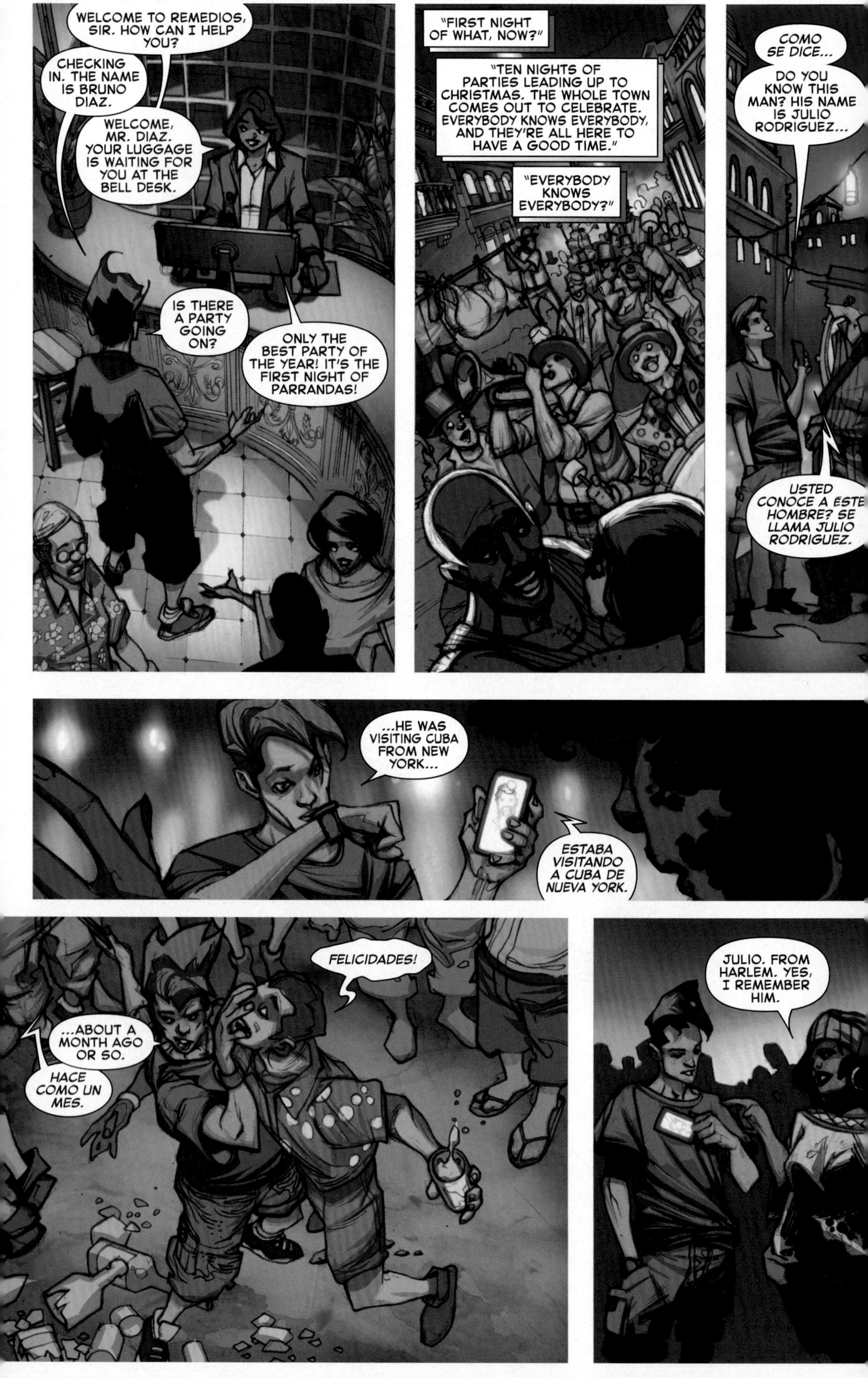
WELCOME TO REMEDIOS, SIR. HOW CAN I HELP YOU?
CHECKING IN. THE NAME IS BRUNO DIAZ.
WELCOME, MR. DIAZ. YOUR LUGGAGE IS WAITING FOR YOU AT THE BELL DESK.
IS THERE A PARTY GOING ON?
ONLY THE BEST PARTY OF THE YEAR! IT'S THE FIRST NIGHT OF PARRANDAS!
"FIRST NIGHT OF WHAT, NOW?"
"TEN NIGHTS OF PARTIES LEADING UP TO CHRISTMAS. THE WHOLE TOWN COMES OUT TO CELEBRATE. EVERYBODY KNOWS EVERYBODY, AND THEY'RE ALL HERE TO HAVE A GOOD TIME."
"EVERYBODY KNOWS EVERYBODY?"
COMO SE DICE...
DO YOU KNOW THIS MAN? HIS NAME IS JULIO RODRIGUEZ...
USTED CONOCE A ESTE HOMBRE? SE LLAMA JULIO RODRIGUEZ.
...HE WAS VISITING CUBA FROM NEW YORK...
ESTABA VISITANDO A CUBA DE NUEVA YORK.
FELICIDADES!
...ABOUT A MONTH AGO OR SO.
HACE COMO UN MES.
JULIO. FROM HARLEM. YES, I REMEMBER HIM.

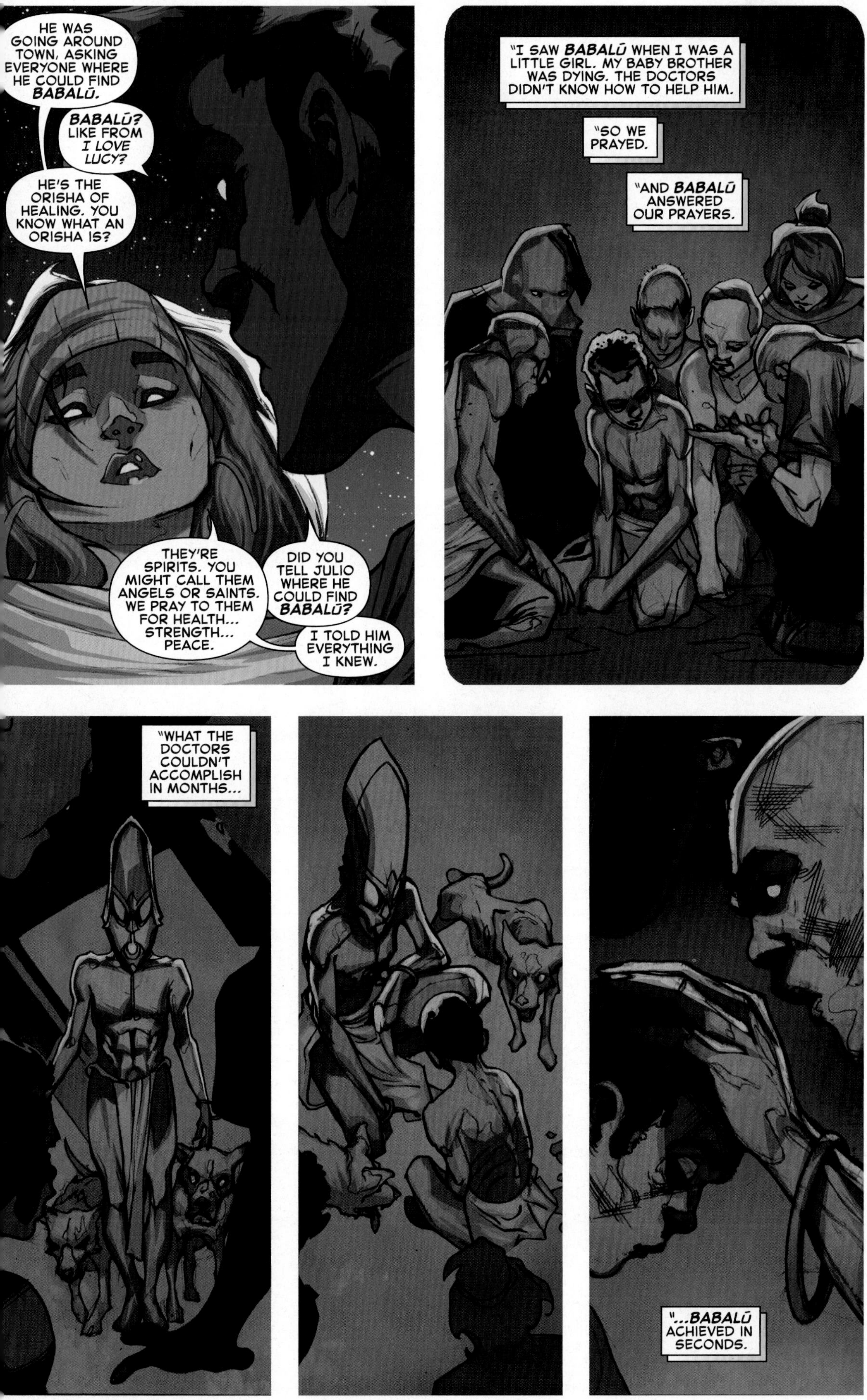
HE WAS GOING AROUND TOWN, ASKING EVERYONE WHERE HE COULD FIND BABALŪ.
BABALŪ? LIKE FROM I LOVE LUCY?
HE'S THE ORISHA OF HEALING. YOU KNOW WHAT AN ORISHA IS?
THEY'RE SPIRITS. YOU MIGHT CALL THEM ANGELS OR SAINTS. WE PRAY TO THEM FOR HEALTH... STRENGTH... PEACE.
DID YOU TELL JULIO WHERE HE COULD FIND BABALŪ?
I TOLD HIM EVERYTHING I KNEW.
"I SAW BABALŪ WHEN I WAS A LITTLE GIRL. MY BABY BROTHER WAS DYING. THE DOCTORS DIDN'T KNOW HOW TO HELP HIM.
"SO WE PRAYED.
"AND BABALŪ ANSWERED OUR PRAYERS.
"WHAT THE DOCTORS COULDN'T ACCOMPLISH IN MONTHS...
"...BABALŪ ACHIEVED IN SECONDS.

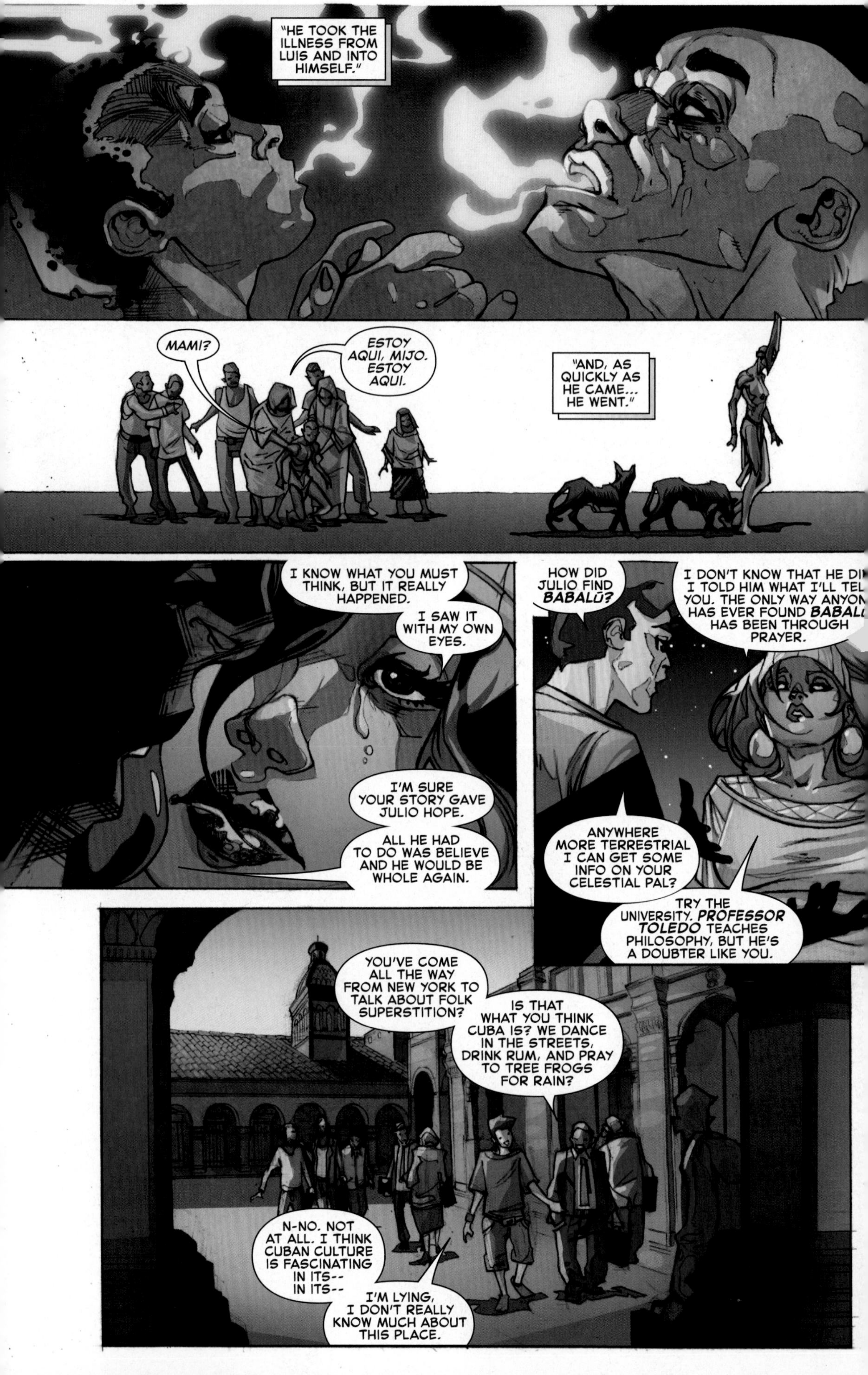
"HE TOOK THE ILLNESS FROM LUIS AND INTO HIMSELF."
MAMI?
ESTOY AQUI, MIJO. ESTOY AQUI.
"AND, AS QUICKLY AS HE CAME... HE WENT."
I KNOW WHAT YOU MUST THINK, BUT IT REALLY HAPPENED.
I SAW IT WITH MY OWN EYES.
I'M SURE YOUR STORY GAVE JULIO HOPE.
ALL HE HAD TO DO WAS BELIEVE AND HE WOULD BE WHOLE AGAIN.
HOW DID JULIO FIND BABALŪ?
I DON'T KNOW THAT HE DI I TOLD HIM WHAT I'LL TEL YOU. THE ONLY WAY ANYON HAS EVER FOUND BABAL HAS BEEN THROUGH PRAYER.
ANYWHERE MORE TERRESTRIAL I CAN GET SOME INFO ON YOUR CELESTIAL PAL?
TRY THE UNIVERSITY. PROFESSOR TOLEDO TEACHES PHILOSOPHY, BUT HE'S A DOUBTER LIKE YOU.
YOU'VE COME ALL THE WAY FROM NEW YORK TO TALK ABOUT FOLK SUPERSTITION?
IS THAT WHAT YOU THINK CUBA IS? WE DANCE IN THE STREETS, DRINK RUM, AND PRAY TO TREE FROGS FOR RAIN?
N-NO. NOT AT ALL. I THINK CUBAN CULTURE IS FASCINATING IN ITS-- IN ITS--
I'M LYING, I DON'T REALLY KNOW MUCH ABOUT THIS PLACE.

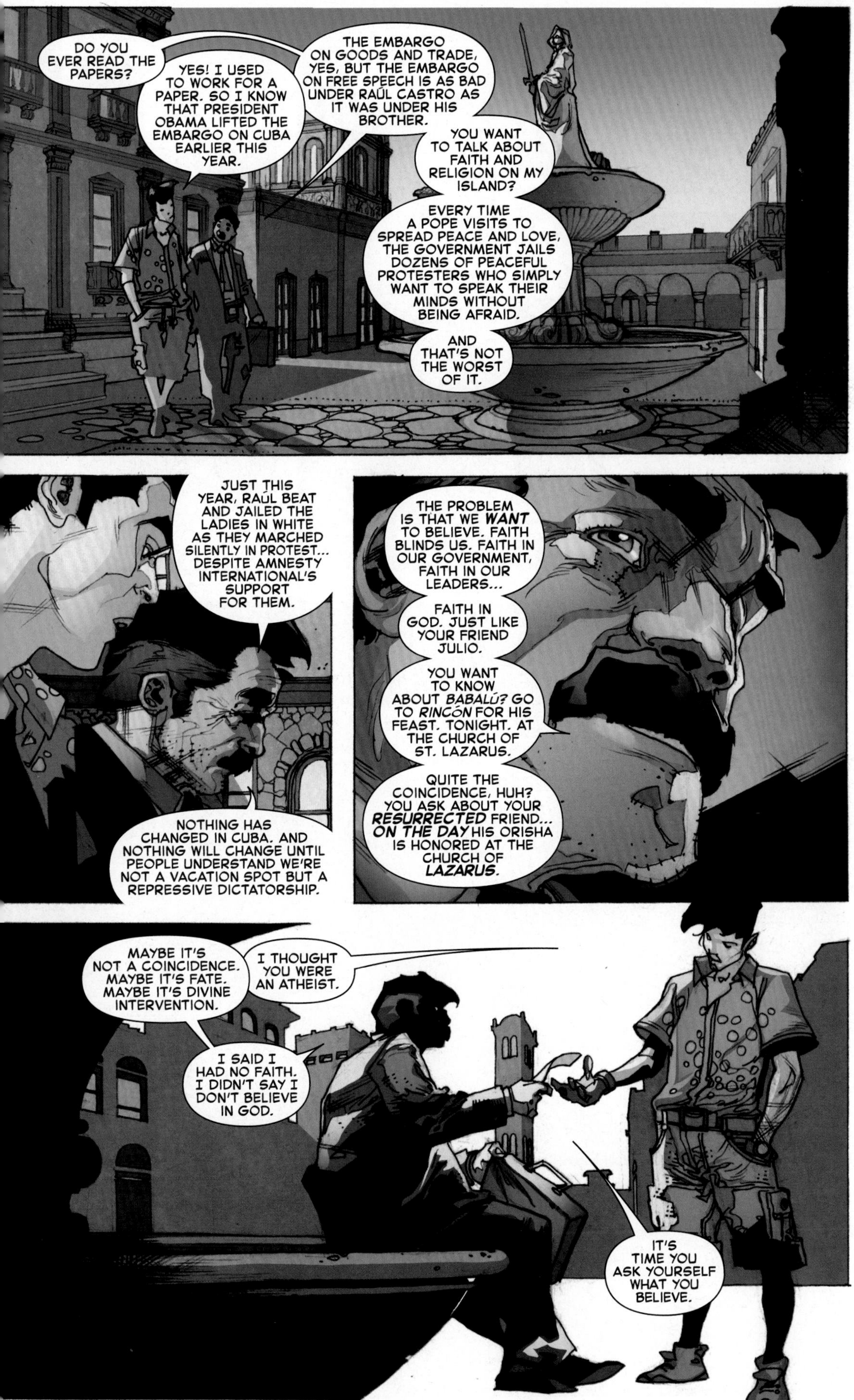
DO YOU EVER READ THE PAPERS?
YES! I USED TO WORK FOR A PAPER. SO I KNOW THAT PRESIDENT OBAMA LIFTED THE EMBARGO ON CUBA EARLIER THIS YEAR.
THE EMBARGO ON GOODS AND TRADE, YES, BUT THE EMBARGO ON FREE SPEECH IS AS BAD UNDER RAÚL CASTRO AS IT WAS UNDER HIS BROTHER.
YOU WANT TO TALK ABOUT FAITH AND RELIGION ON MY ISLAND?
EVERY TIME A POPE VISITS TO SPREAD PEACE AND LOVE, THE GOVERNMENT JAILS DOZENS OF PEACEFUL PROTESTERS WHO SIMPLY WANT TO SPEAK THEIR MINDS WITHOUT BEING AFRAID.
AND THAT'S NOT THE WORST OF IT.
JUST THIS YEAR, RAÚL BEAT AND JAILED THE LADIES IN WHITE AS THEY MARCHED SILENTLY IN PROTEST... DESPITE AMNESTY INTERNATIONAL'S SUPPORT FOR THEM.
NOTHING HAS CHANGED IN CUBA. AND NOTHING WILL CHANGE UNTIL PEOPLE UNDERSTAND WE'RE NOT A VACATION SPOT BUT A REPRESSIVE DICTATORSHIP.
THE PROBLEM IS THAT WE *WANT* TO BELIEVE. FAITH BLINDS US. FAITH IN OUR GOVERNMENT, FAITH IN OUR LEADERS...
FAITH IN GOD. JUST LIKE YOUR FRIEND JULIO.
YOU WANT TO KNOW ABOUT *BABALÚ?* GO TO *RINCÓN* FOR HIS FEAST. TONIGHT. AT THE CHURCH OF ST. LAZARUS.
QUITE THE COINCIDENCE, HUH? YOU ASK ABOUT YOUR ***RESURRECTED*** FRIEND... ***ON THE DAY*** HIS ORISHA IS HONORED AT THE CHURCH OF ***LAZARUS***.
MAYBE IT'S NOT A COINCIDENCE. MAYBE IT'S FATE. MAYBE IT'S DIVINE INTERVENTION.
I THOUGHT YOU WERE AN ATHEIST.
I SAID I HAD NO FAITH. I DIDN'T SAY I DON'T BELIEVE IN GOD.
IT'S TIME YOU ASK YOURSELF WHAT YOU BELIEVE.

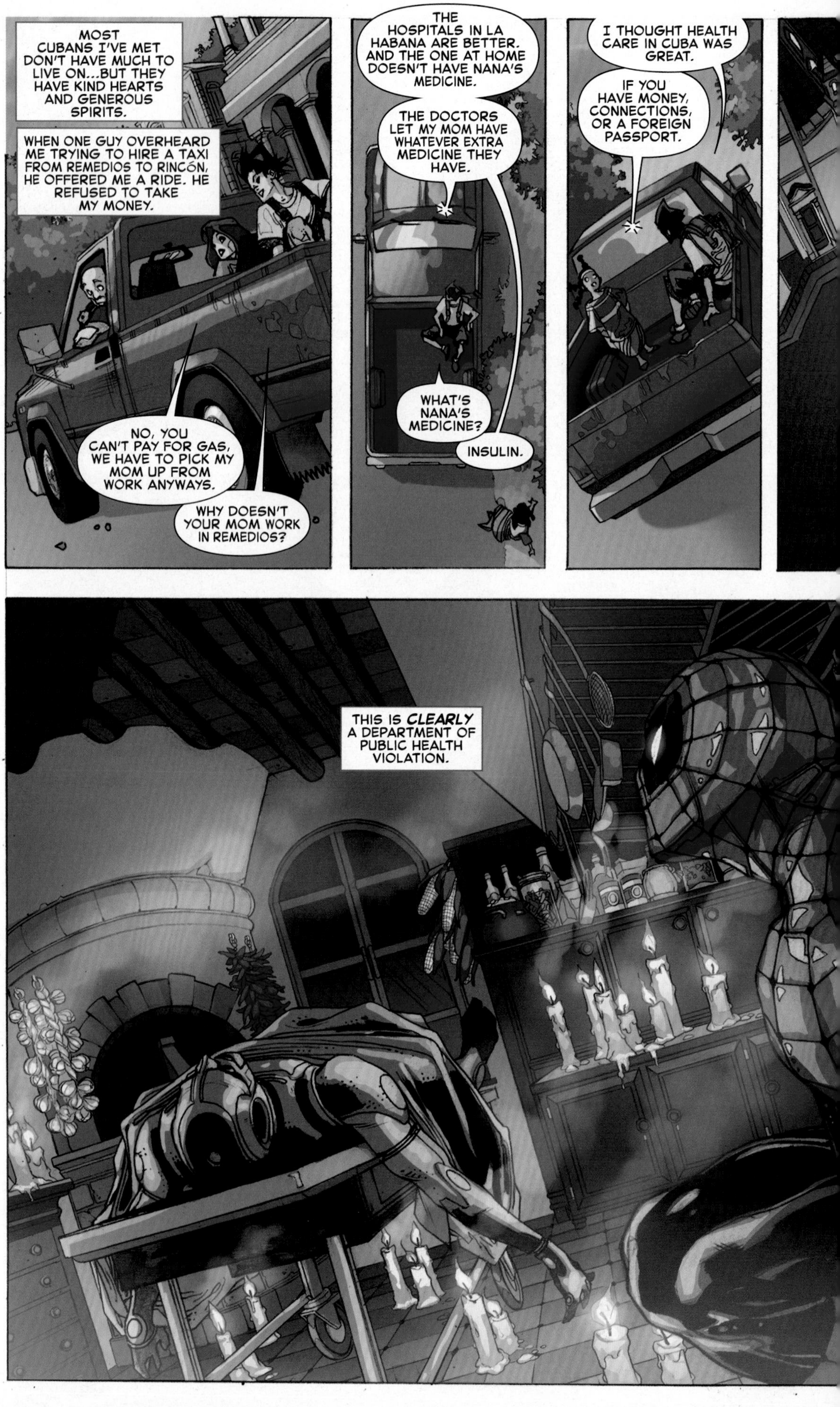

MOST CUBANS I'VE MET DON'T HAVE MUCH TO LIVE ON...BUT THEY HAVE KIND HEARTS AND GENEROUS SPIRITS.
WHEN ONE GUY OVERHEARD ME TRYING TO HIRE A TAXI FROM REMEDIOS TO RINCÓN, HE OFFERED ME A RIDE. HE REFUSED TO TAKE MY MONEY.
NO, YOU CAN'T PAY FOR GAS, WE HAVE TO PICK MY MOM UP FROM WORK ANYWAYS.
WHY DOESN'T YOUR MOM WORK IN REMEDIOS?
THE HOSPITALS IN LA HABANA ARE BETTER. AND THE ONE AT HOME DOESN'T HAVE NANA'S MEDICINE.
THE DOCTORS LET MY MOM HAVE WHATEVER EXTRA MEDICINE THEY HAVE.
WHAT'S NANA'S MEDICINE?
INSULIN.
I THOUGHT HEALTH CARE IN CUBA WAS GREAT.
IF YOU HAVE MONEY, CONNECTIONS, OR A FOREIGN PASSPORT.
THIS IS CLEARLY A DEPARTMENT OF PUBLIC HEALTH VIOLATION.

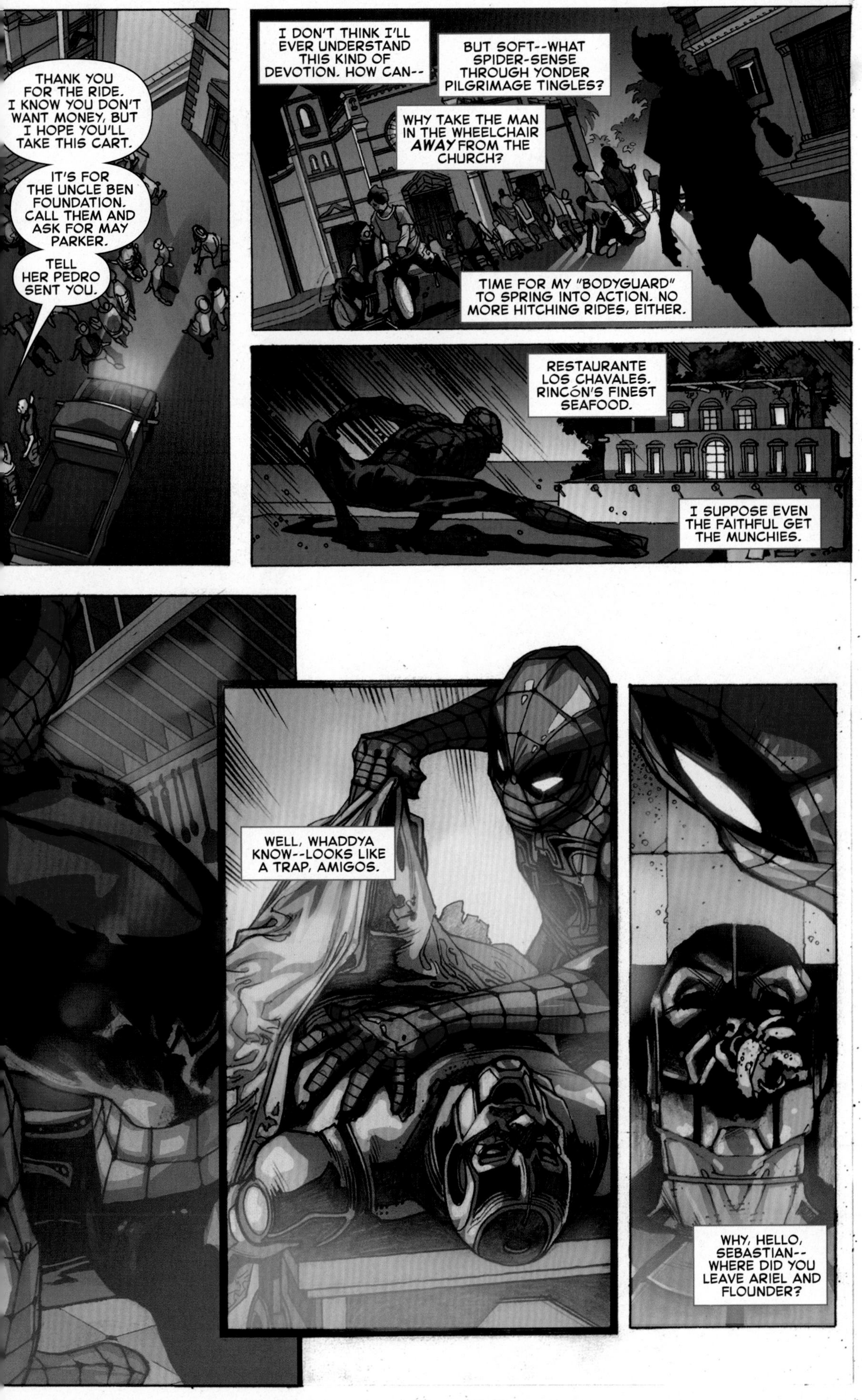
THANK YOU FOR THE RIDE. I KNOW YOU DON'T WANT MONEY, BUT I HOPE YOU'LL TAKE THIS CART.
IT'S FOR THE UNCLE BEN FOUNDATION. CALL THEM AND ASK FOR MAY PARKER.
TELL HER PEDRO SENT YOU.
I DON'T THINK I'LL EVER UNDERSTAND THIS KIND OF DEVOTION. HOW CAN--
BUT SOFT--WHAT SPIDER-SENSE THROUGH YONDER PILGRIMAGE TINGLES?
WHY TAKE THE MAN IN THE WHEELCHAIR *AWAY* FROM THE CHURCH?
TIME FOR MY "BODYGUARD" TO SPRING INTO ACTION. NO MORE HITCHING RIDES, EITHER.
RESTAURANTE LOS CHAVALES. RINCÓN'S FINEST SEAFOOD.
I SUPPOSE EVEN THE FAITHFUL GET THE MUNCHIES.
WELL, WHADDYA KNOW--LOOKS LIKE A TRAP, AMIGOS.
WHY, HELLO, SEBASTIAN--WHERE DID YOU LEAVE ARIEL AND FLOUNDER?

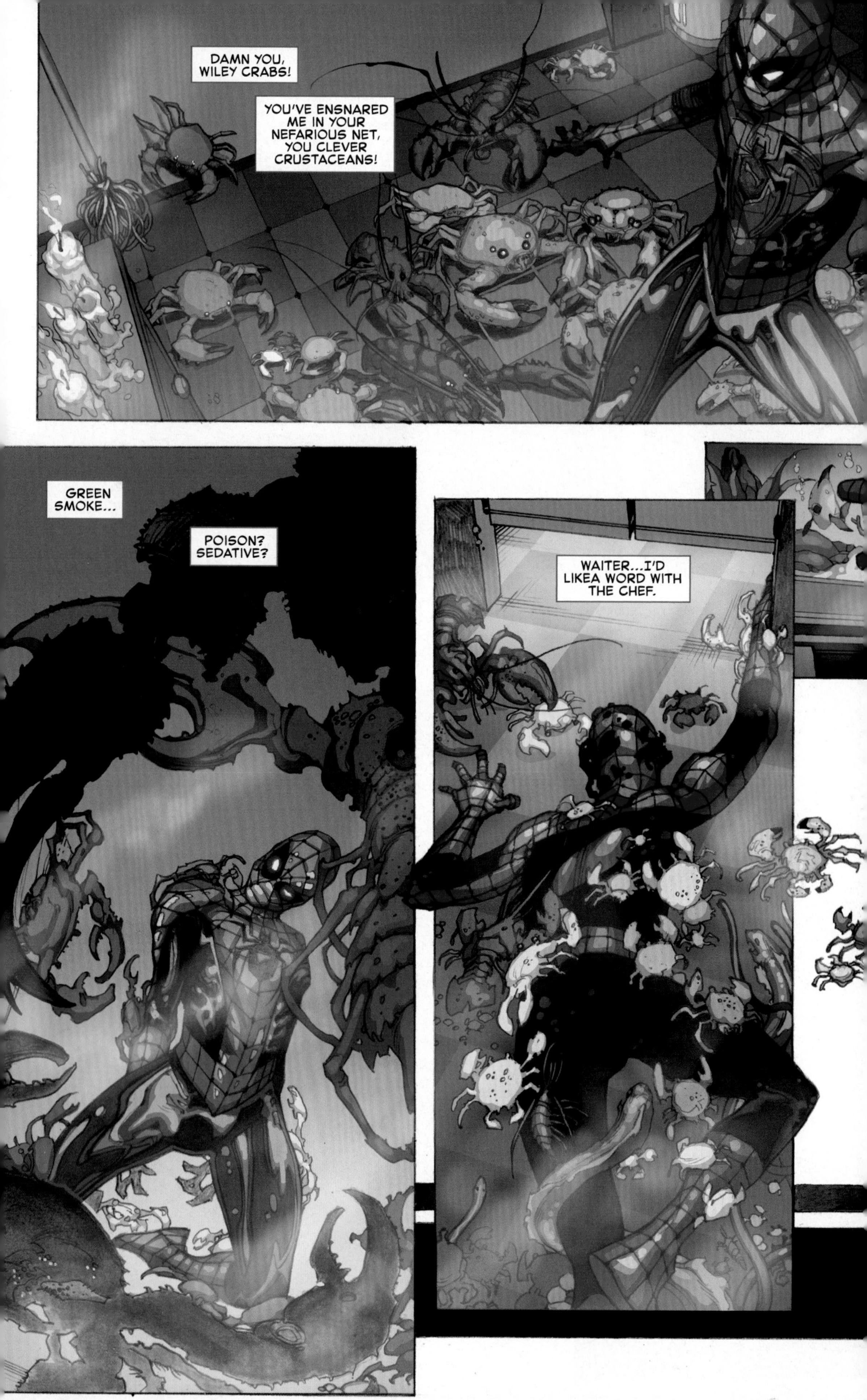
DAMN YOU, WILEY CRABS!
YOU'VE ENSNARED ME IN YOUR NEFARIOUS NET, YOU CLEVER CRUSTACEANS!
GREEN SMOKE...
POISON? SEDATIVE?
WAITER...I'D LIKEA WORD WITH THE CHEF.

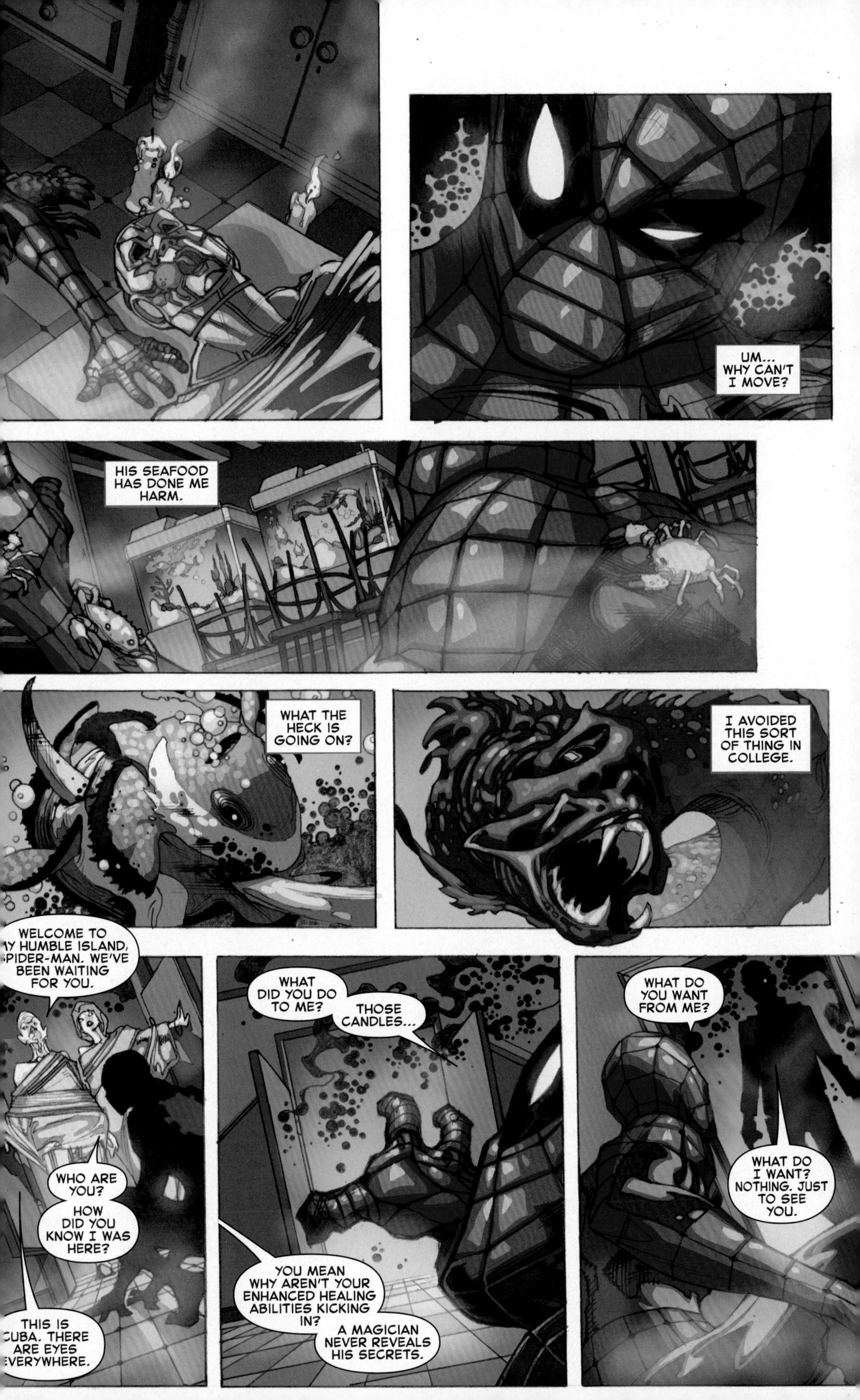
UM... WHY CAN'T I MOVE?
HIS SEAFOOD HAS DONE ME HARM.
WHAT THE HECK IS GOING ON?
I AVOIDED THIS SORT OF THING IN COLLEGE.
WELCOME TO MY HUMBLE ISLAND, SPIDER-MAN. WE'VE BEEN WAITING FOR YOU.
WHO ARE YOU?
HOW DID YOU KNOW I WAS HERE?
THIS IS CUBA. THERE ARE EYES EVERYWHERE.
WHAT DID YOU DO TO ME?
THOSE CANDLES...
YOU MEAN WHY AREN'T YOUR ENHANCED HEALING ABILITIES KICKING IN?
A MAGICIAN NEVER REVEALS HIS SECRETS.
WHAT DO YOU WANT FROM ME?
WHAT DO I WANT? NOTHING. JUST TO SEE YOU.

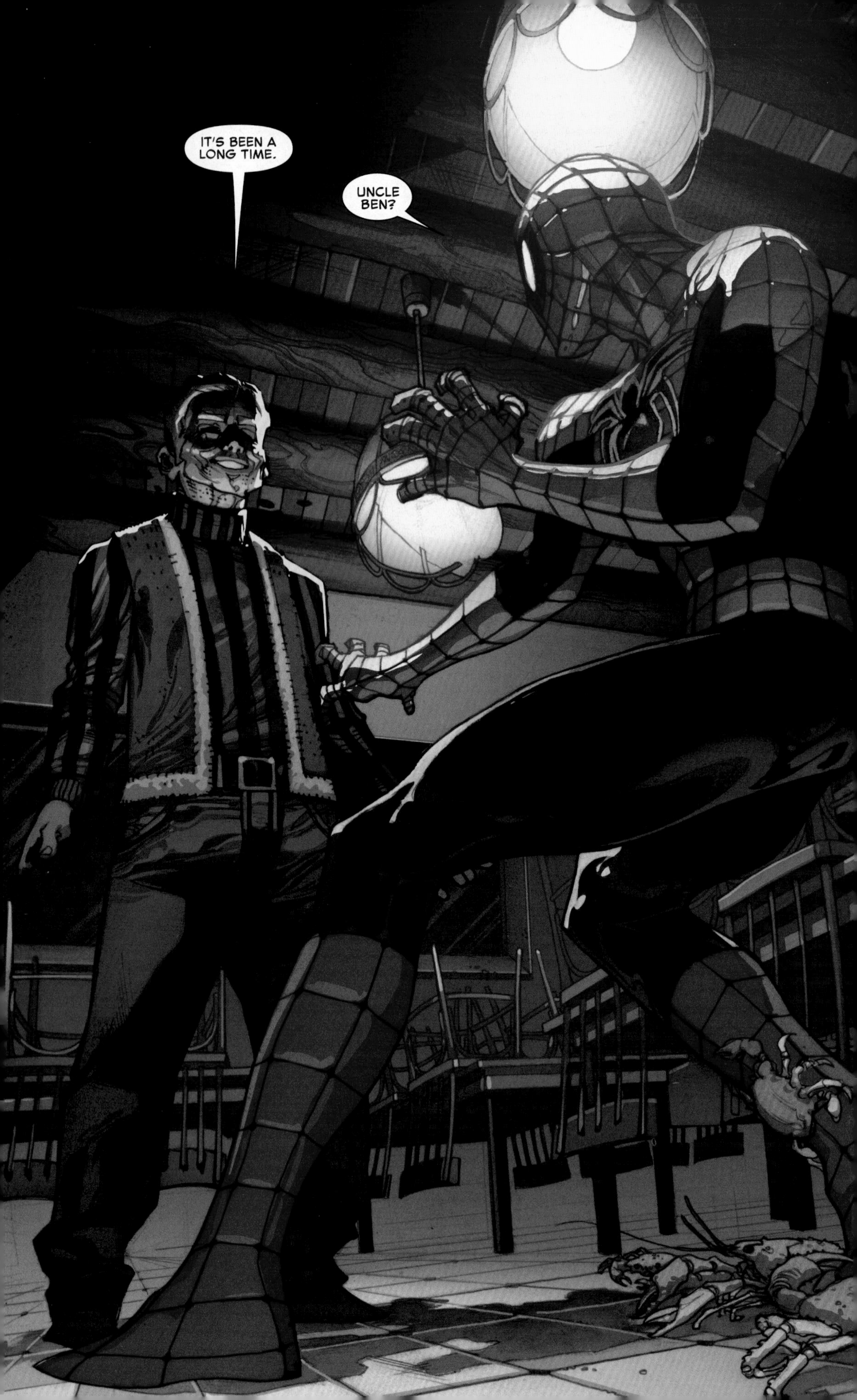
IT'S BEEN A LONG TIME.
UNCLE BEN?

1.3

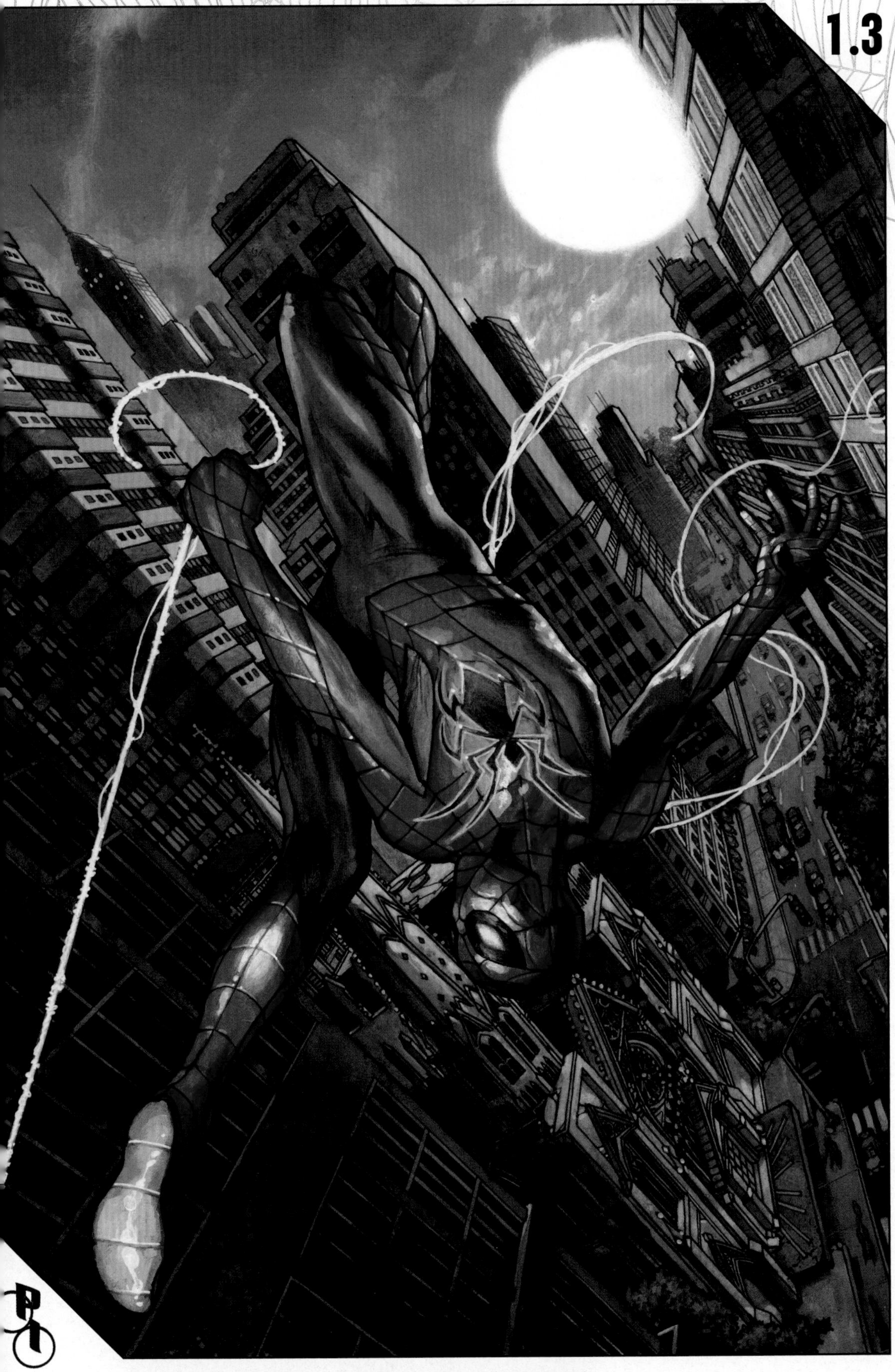

"DANGERS, TOILS AND SNARES"

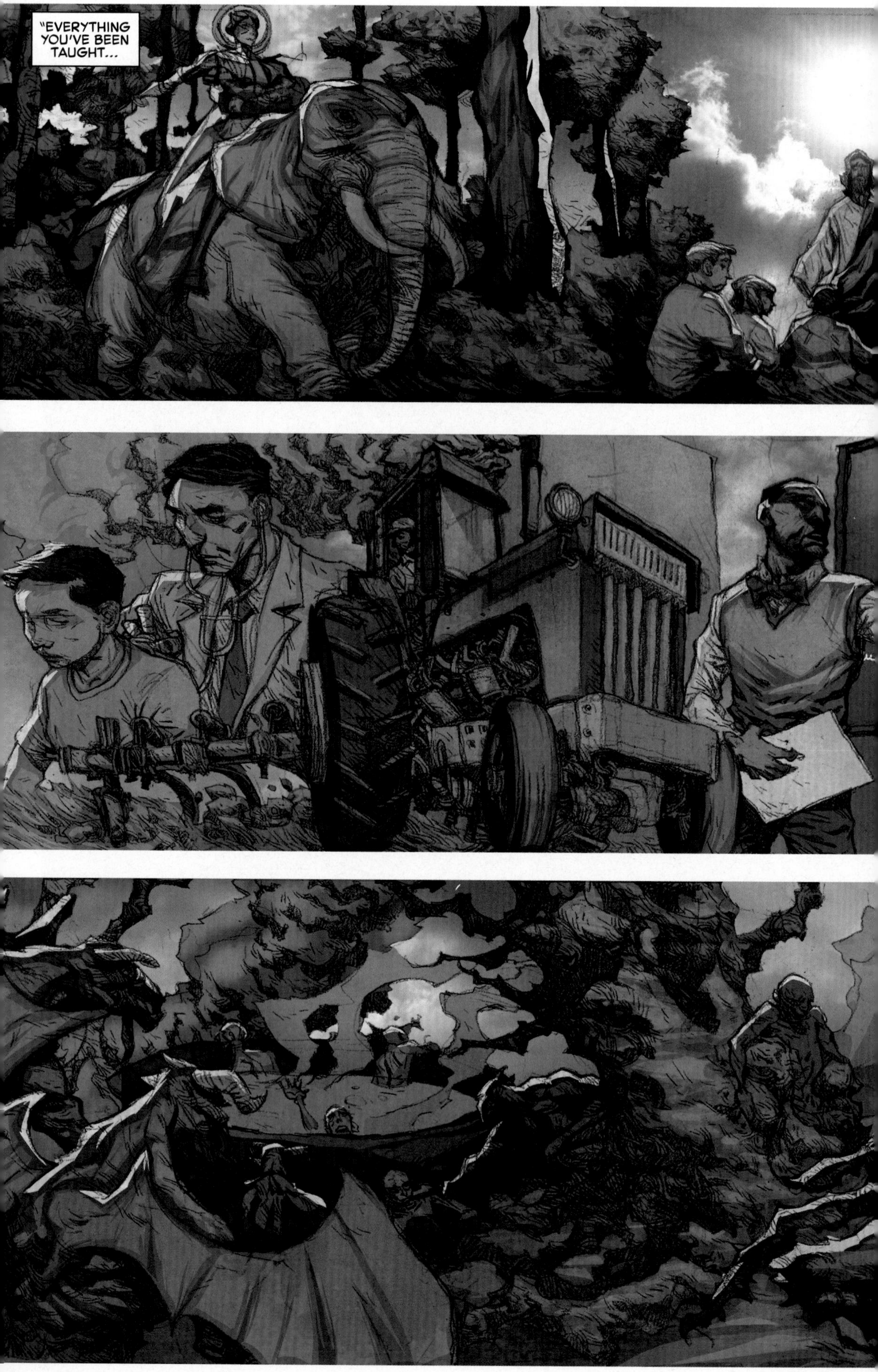
"EVERYTHING YOU'VE BEEN TAUGHT...

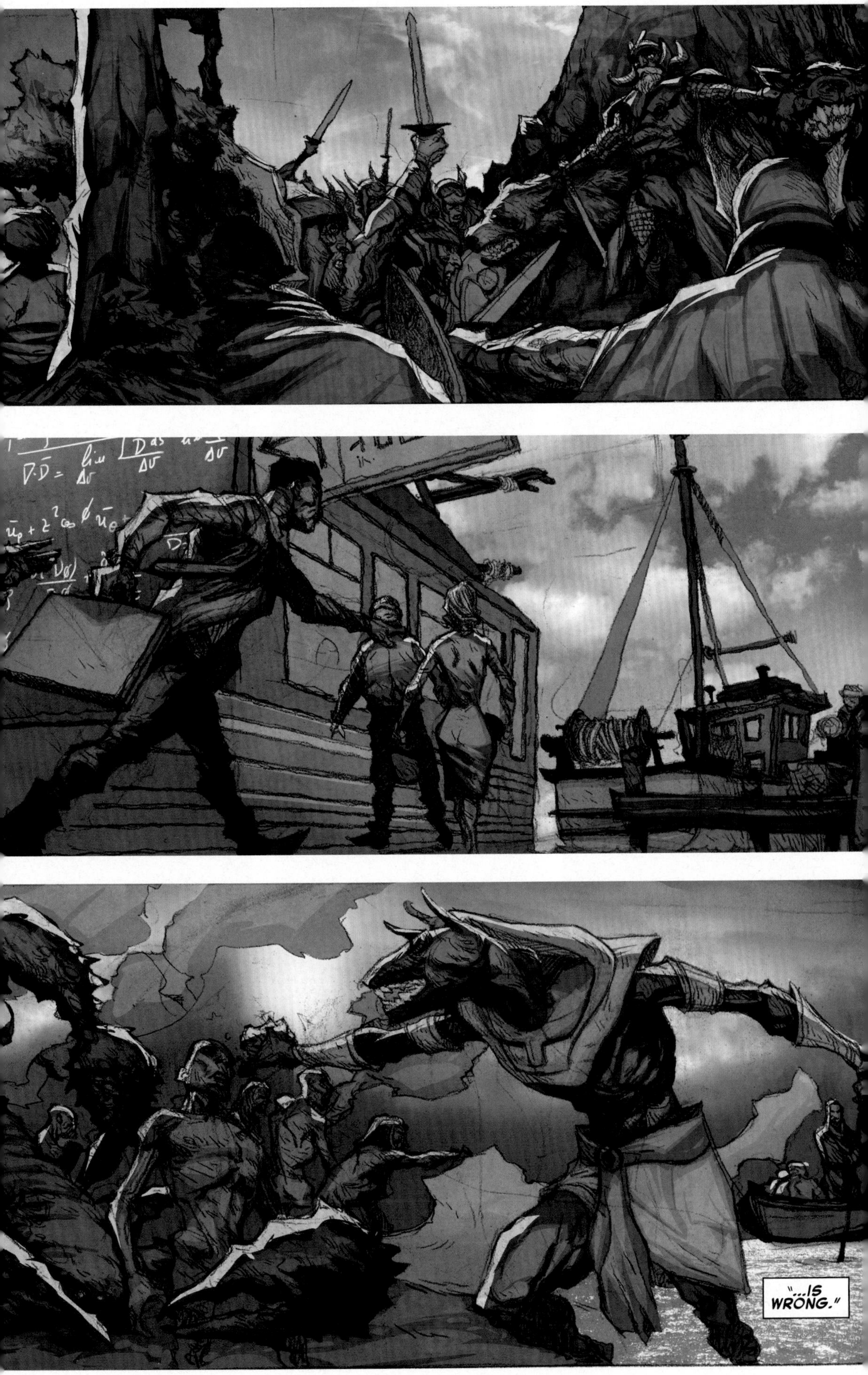
"...IS WRONG."

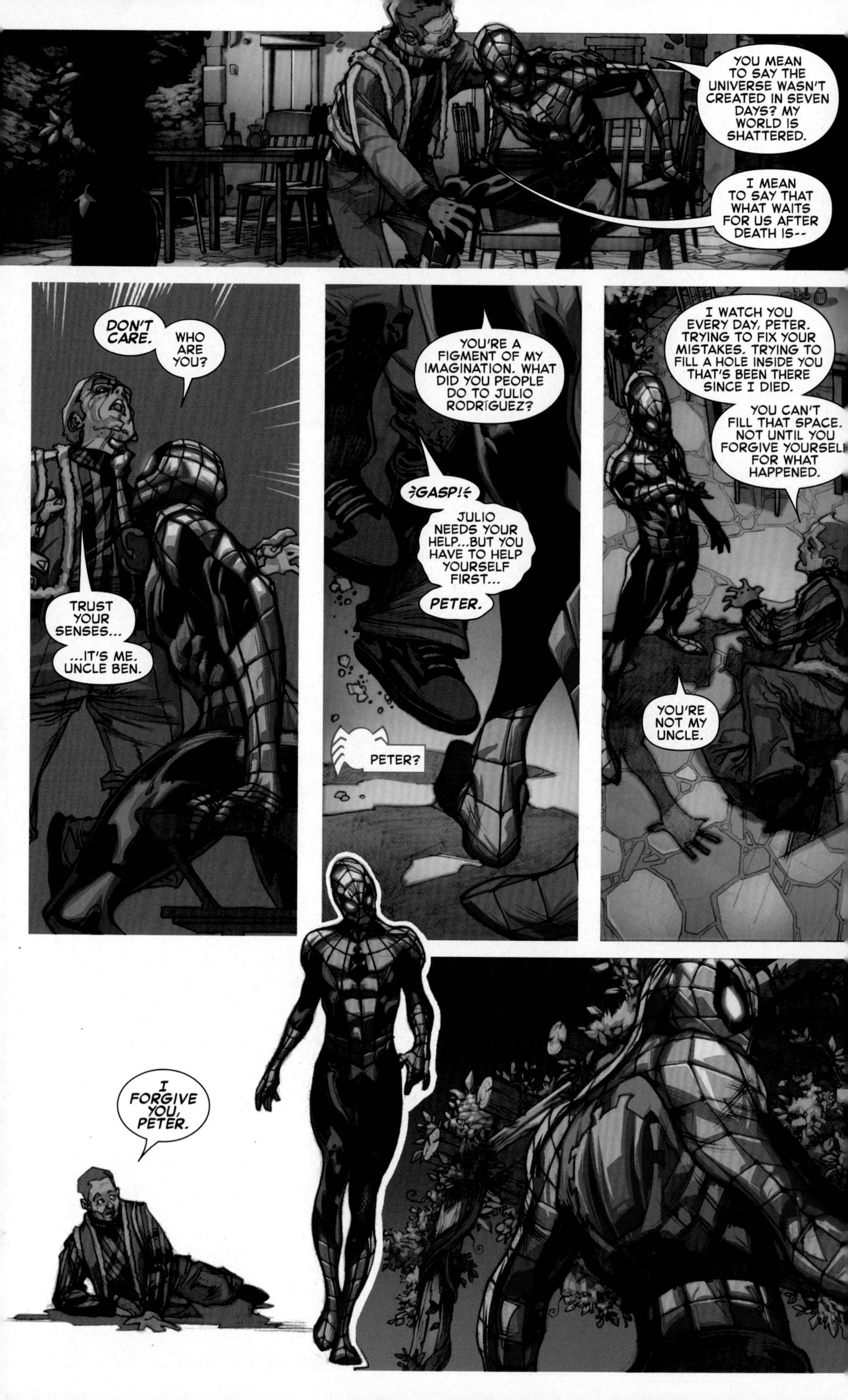

YOU MEAN TO SAY THE UNIVERSE WASN'T CREATED IN SEVEN DAYS? MY WORLD IS SHATTERED.
I MEAN TO SAY THAT WHAT WAITS FOR US AFTER DEATH IS--
DON'T CARE.
WHO ARE YOU?
TRUST YOUR SENSES...
...IT'S ME. UNCLE BEN.
YOU'RE A FIGMENT OF MY IMAGINATION. WHAT DID YOU PEOPLE DO TO JULIO RODRÍGUEZ?
GASP!
JULIO NEEDS YOUR HELP...BUT YOU HAVE TO HELP YOURSELF FIRST...
PETER.
PETER?
I WATCH YOU EVERY DAY, PETER. TRYING TO FIX YOUR MISTAKES. TRYING TO FILL A HOLE INSIDE YOU THAT'S BEEN THERE SINCE I DIED.
YOU CAN'T FILL THAT SPACE. NOT UNTIL YOU FORGIVE YOURSELF FOR WHAT HAPPENED.
YOU'RE NOT MY UNCLE.
I FORGIVE YOU, PETER.

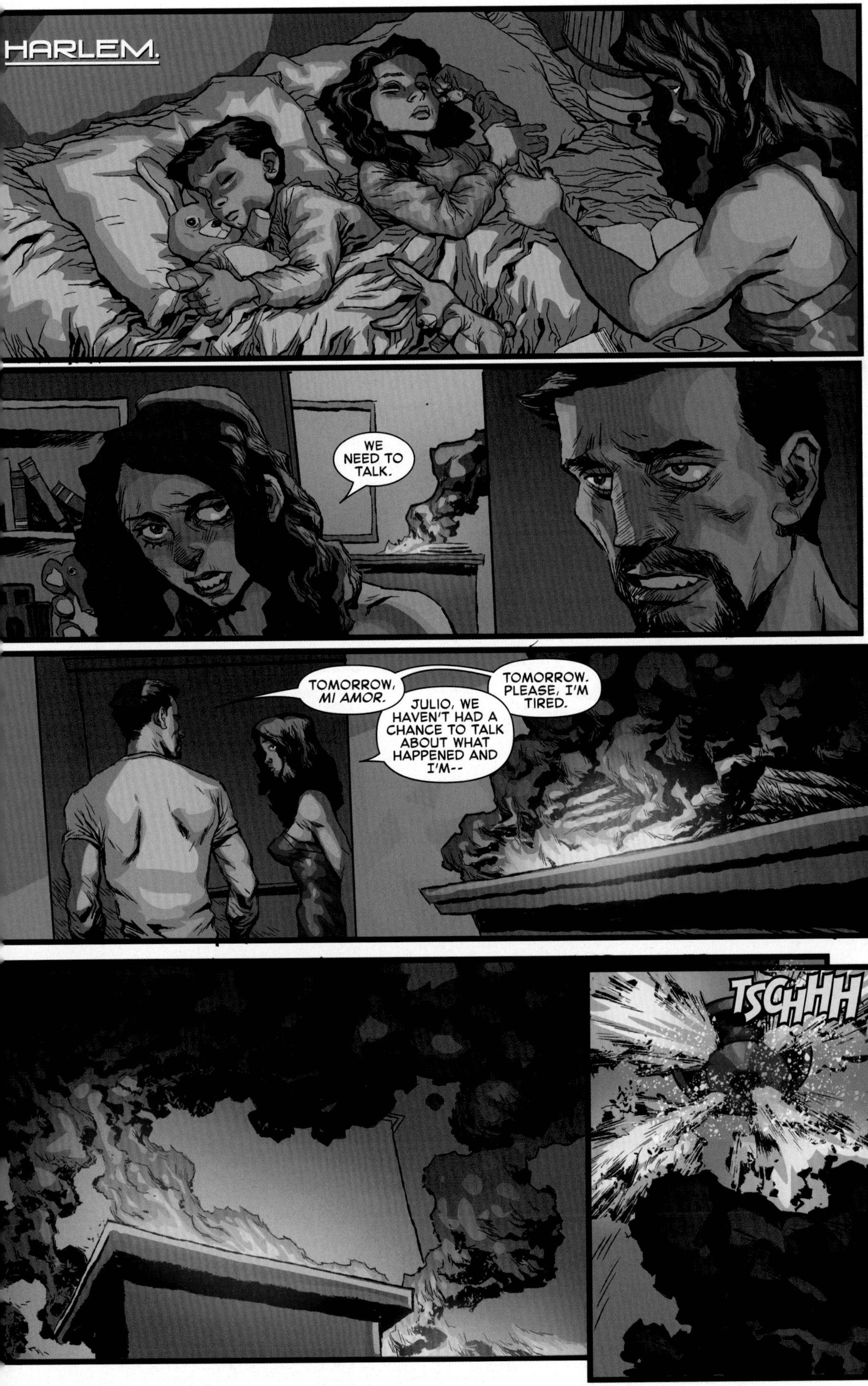
HARLEM.
WE NEED TO TALK.
TOMORROW, MI AMOR.
JULIO, WE HAVEN'T HAD A CHANCE TO TALK ABOUT WHAT HAPPENED AND I'M--
TOMORROW. PLEASE, I'M TIRED.
TSCHHH

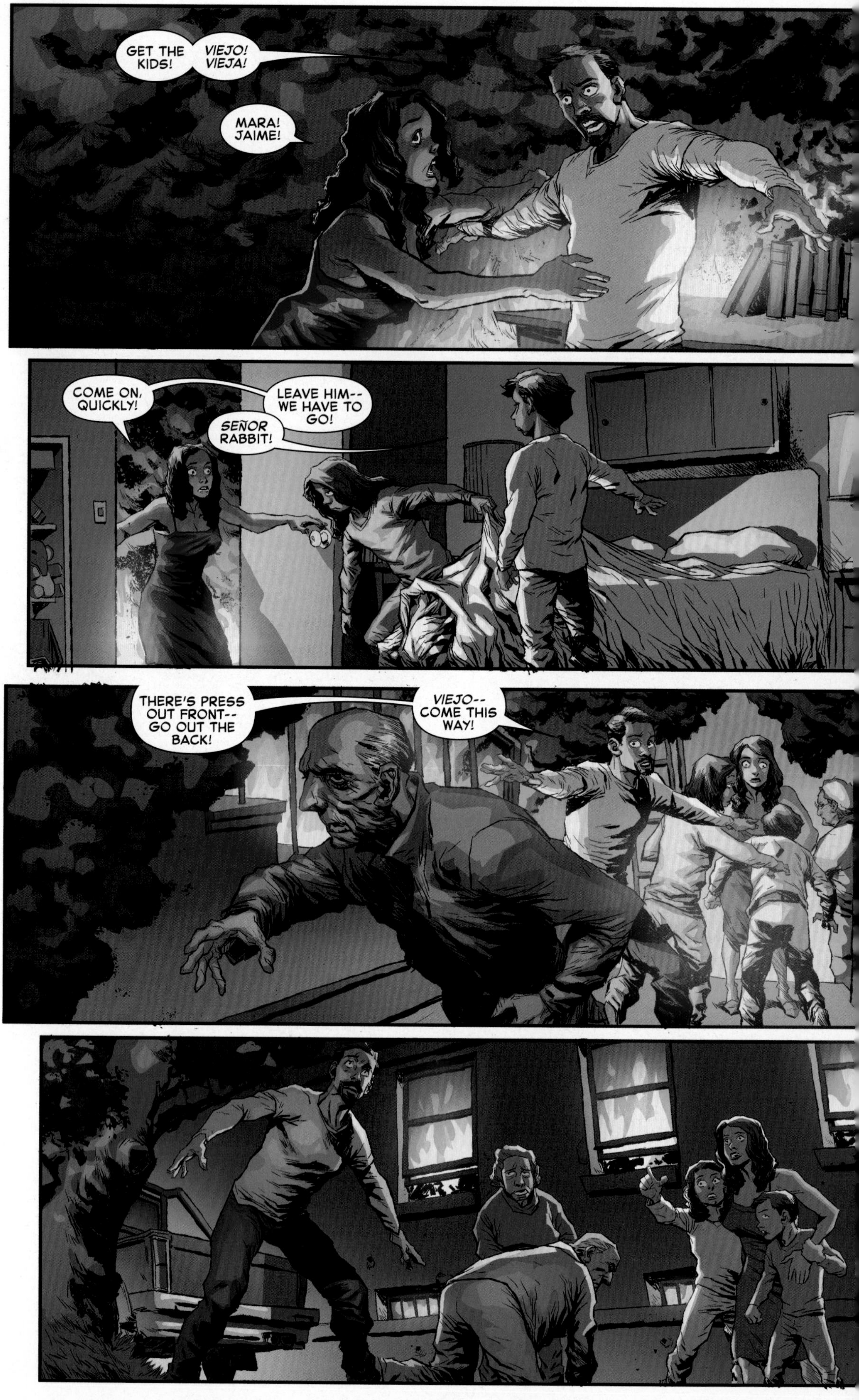
GET THE KIDS!
VIEJO! VIEJA!
MARA! JAIME!
COME ON, QUICKLY!
LEAVE HIM-- WE HAVE TO GO!
SEÑOR RABBIT!
THERE'S PRESS OUT FRONT-- GO OUT THE BACK!
VIEJO-- COME THIS WAY!

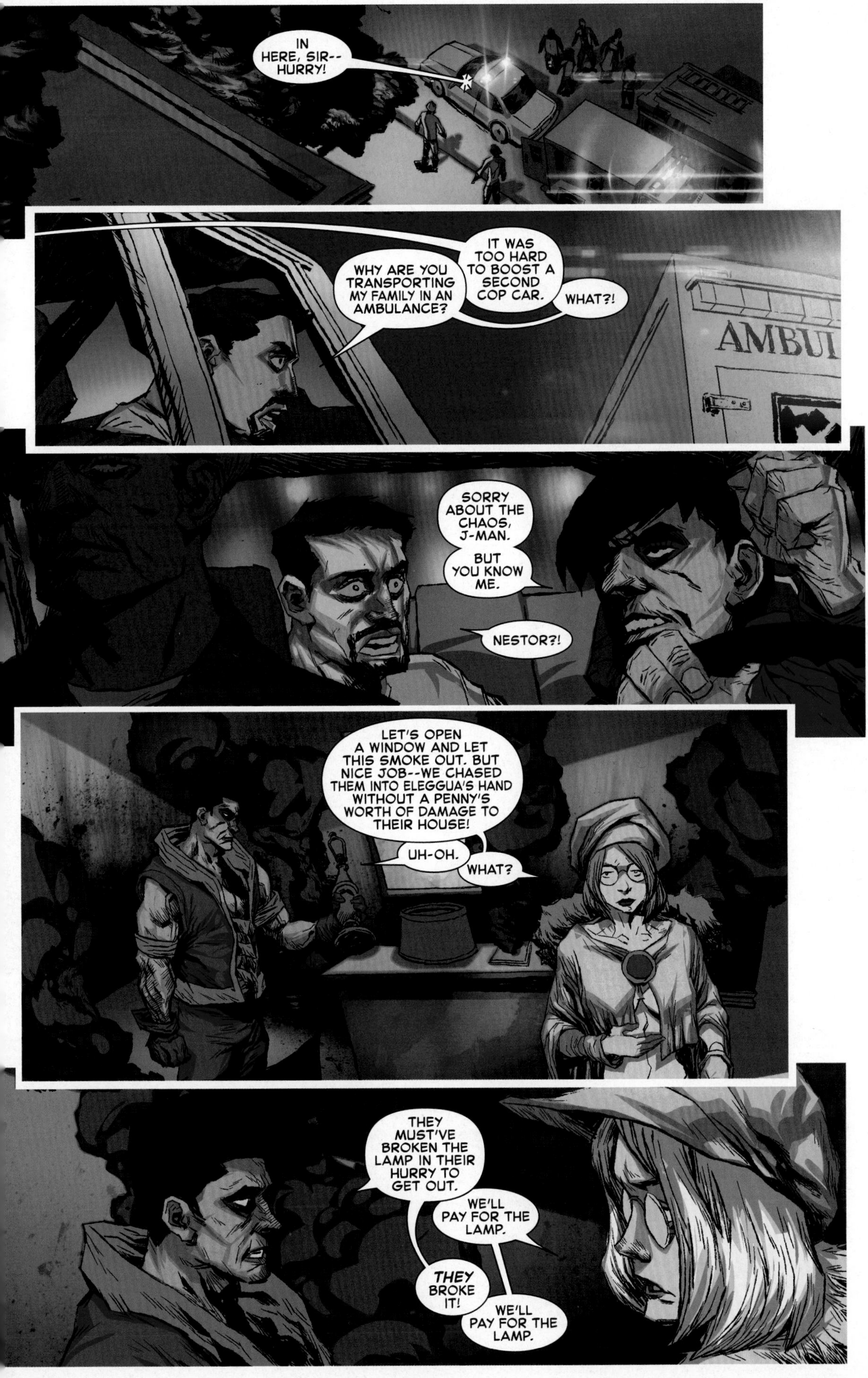
IN HERE, SIR-- HURRY!
WHY ARE YOU TRANSPORTING MY FAMILY IN AN AMBULANCE?
IT WAS TOO HARD TO BOOST A SECOND COP CAR.
WHAT?!
AMBUL
SORRY ABOUT THE CHAOS, J-MAN.
BUT YOU KNOW ME.
NESTOR?!
LET'S OPEN A WINDOW AND LET THIS SMOKE OUT. BUT NICE JOB--WE CHASED THEM INTO ELEGGUA'S HAND WITHOUT A PENNY'S WORTH OF DAMAGE TO THEIR HOUSE!
UH-OH.
WHAT?
THEY MUST'VE BROKEN THE LAMP IN THEIR HURRY TO GET OUT.
WE'LL PAY FOR THE LAMP.
THEY BROKE IT!
WE'LL PAY FOR THE LAMP.

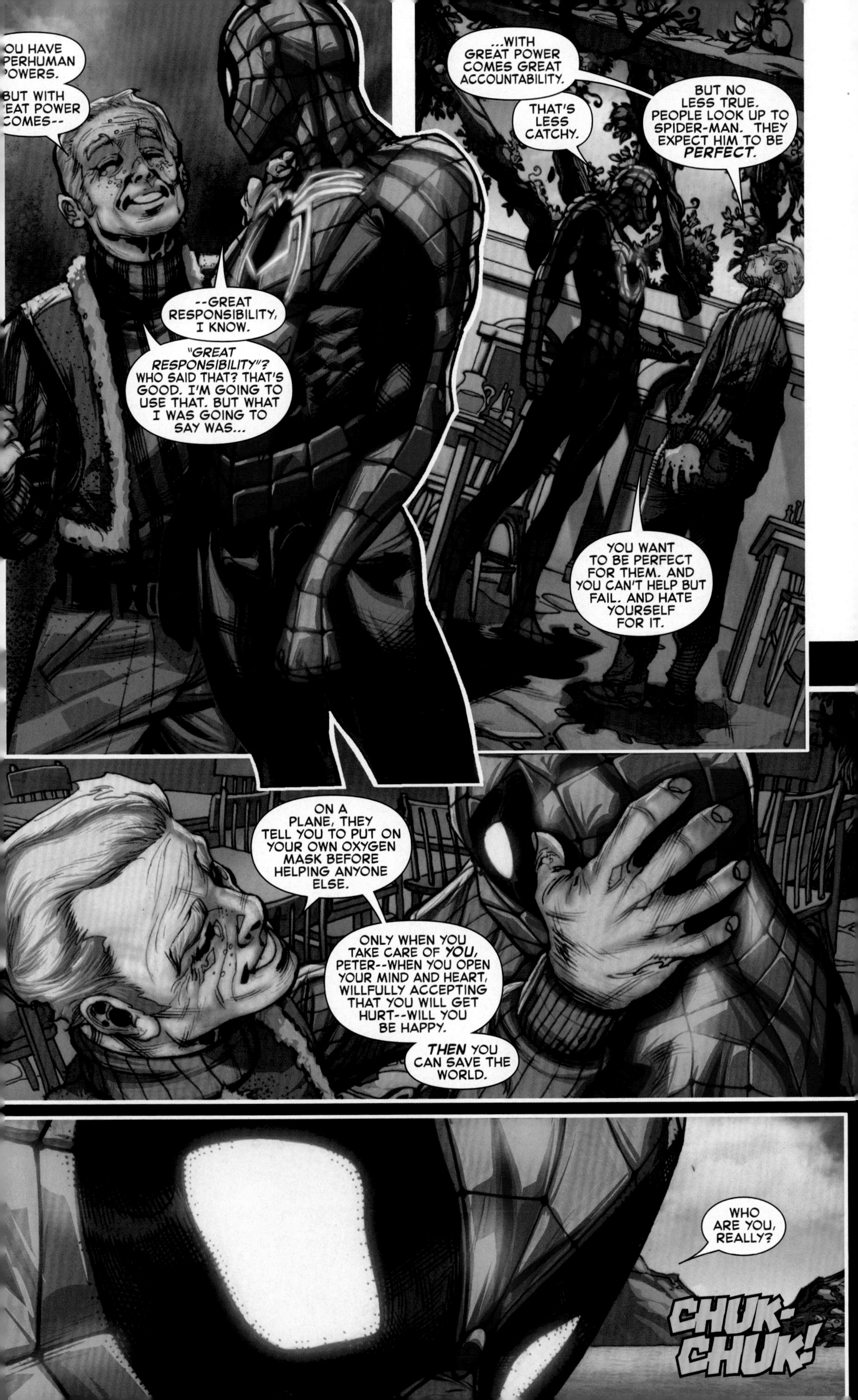
OU HAVE
PERHUMAN
POWERS.
BUT WITH
EAT POWER
COMES--
--GREAT RESPONSIBILITY, I KNOW.
"GREAT RESPONSIBILITY"? WHO SAID THAT? THAT'S GOOD. I'M GOING TO USE THAT. BUT WHAT I WAS GOING TO SAY WAS...
...WITH GREAT POWER COMES GREAT ACCOUNTABILITY.
THAT'S LESS CATCHY.
BUT NO LESS TRUE. PEOPLE LOOK UP TO SPIDER-MAN. THEY EXPECT HIM TO BE *PERFECT*.
YOU WANT TO BE PERFECT FOR THEM. AND YOU CAN'T HELP BUT FAIL. AND HATE YOURSELF FOR IT.
ON A PLANE, THEY TELL YOU TO PUT ON YOUR OWN OXYGEN MASK BEFORE HELPING ANYONE ELSE.
ONLY WHEN YOU TAKE CARE OF *YOU*, PETER--WHEN YOU OPEN YOUR MIND AND HEART, WILLFULLY ACCEPTING THAT YOU WILL GET HURT--WILL YOU BE HAPPY.
THEN YOU CAN SAVE THE WORLD.
WHO ARE YOU, REALLY?
CHUK-CHUK!

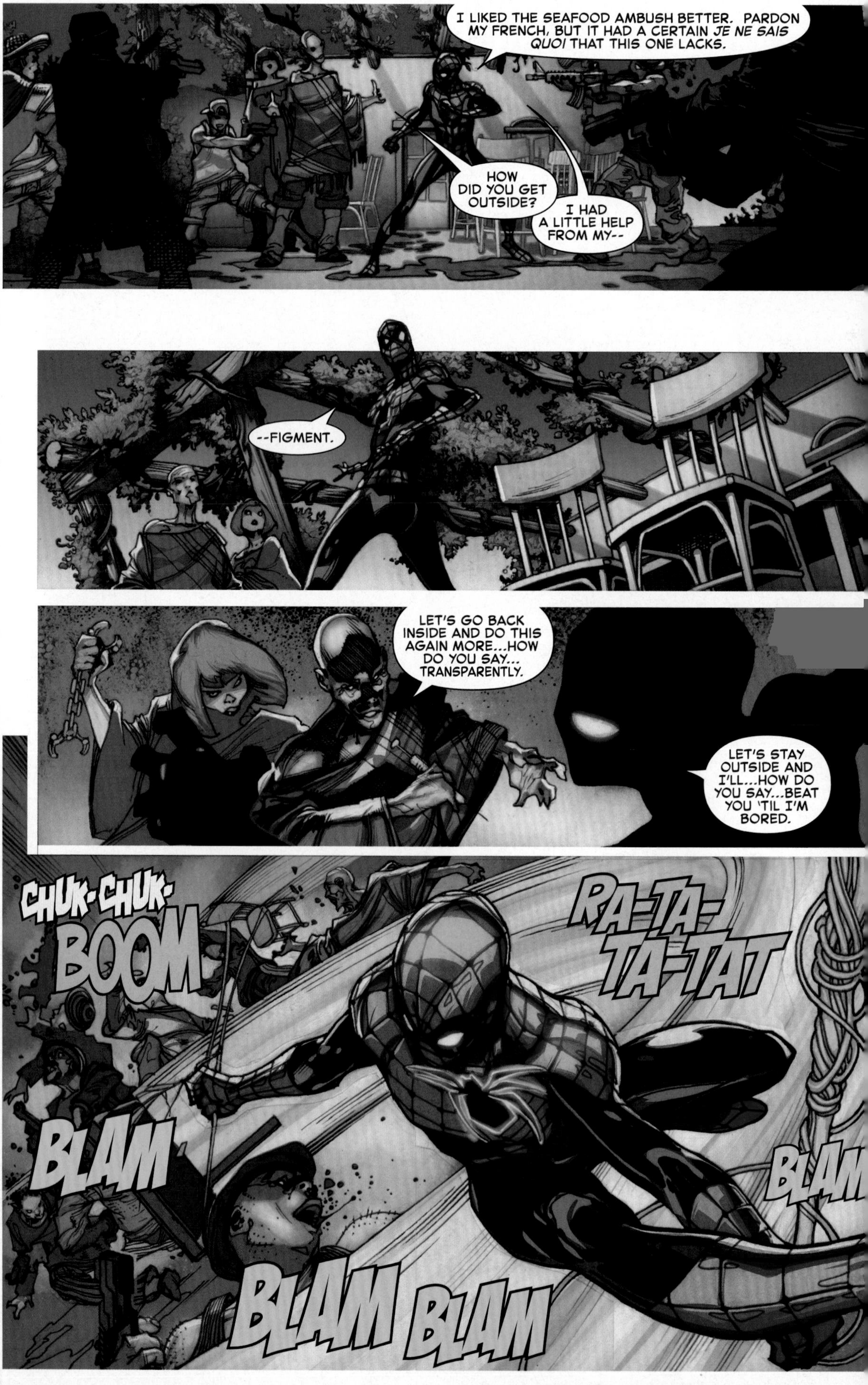
I LIKED THE SEAFOOD AMBUSH BETTER. PARDON MY FRENCH, BUT IT HAD A CERTAIN *JE NE SAIS QUOI* THAT THIS ONE LACKS.
HOW DID YOU GET OUTSIDE?
I HAD A LITTLE HELP FROM MY--
--FIGMENT.
LET'S GO BACK INSIDE AND DO THIS AGAIN MORE...HOW DO YOU SAY... TRANSPARENTLY.
LET'S STAY OUTSIDE AND I'LL...HOW DO YOU SAY...BEAT YOU 'TIL I'M BORED.
CHUK-CHUK-BOOM
RA-TA-TA-TAT
BLAM
BLAM
BLAM BLAM

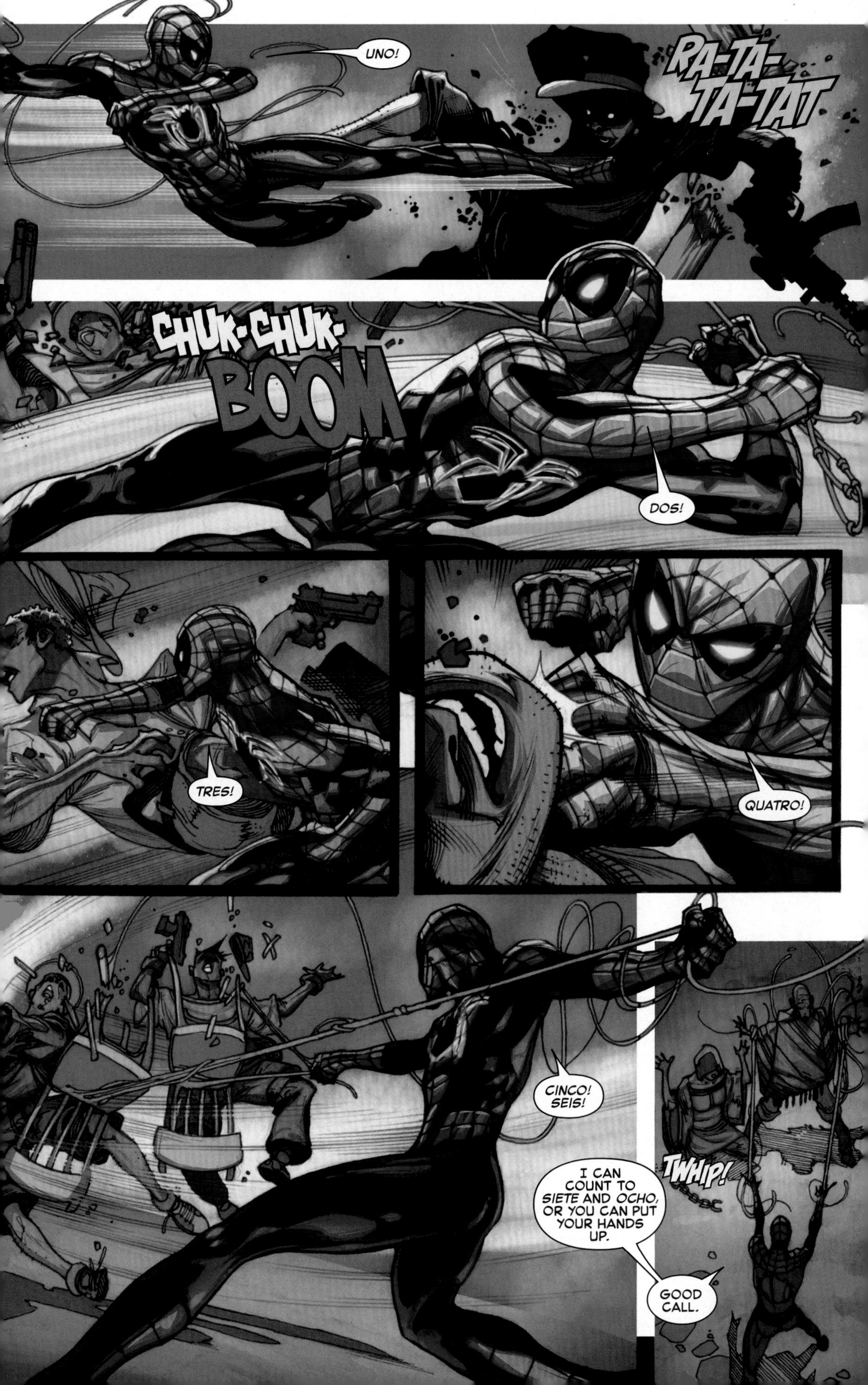
UNO!
RA-TA-TA-TAT
CHUK-CHUK-BOOM
DOS!
TRES!
QUATRO!
CINCO! SEIS!
TWHIP!
I CAN COUNT TO SIETE AND OCHO, OR YOU CAN PUT YOUR HANDS UP.
GOOD CALL.

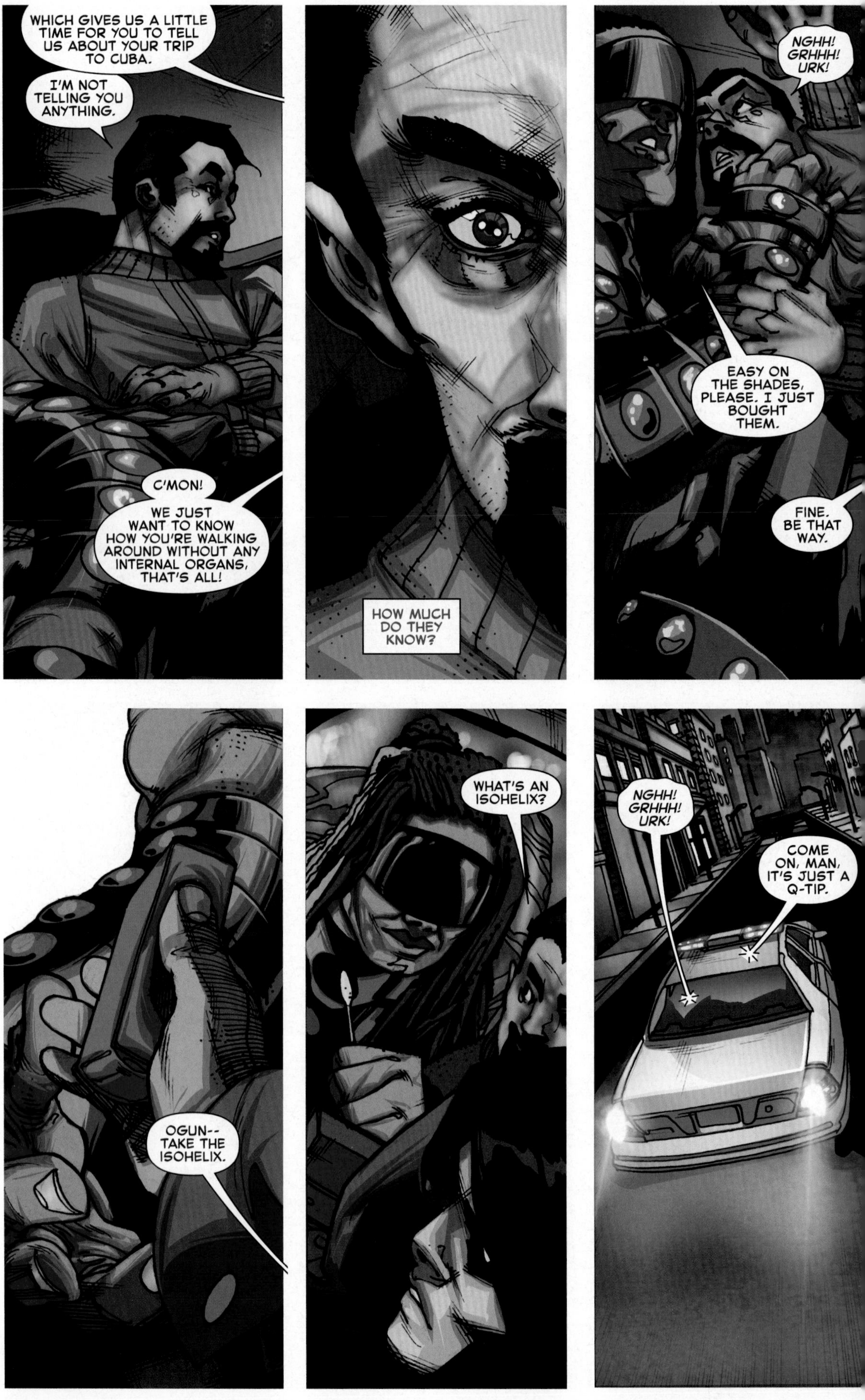
WHICH GIVES US A LITTLE TIME FOR YOU TO TELL US ABOUT YOUR TRIP TO CUBA.
I'M NOT TELLING YOU ANYTHING.
C'MON!
WE JUST WANT TO KNOW HOW YOU'RE WALKING AROUND WITHOUT ANY INTERNAL ORGANS, THAT'S ALL!
HOW MUCH DO THEY KNOW?
NGHH! GRHHH! URK!
EASY ON THE SHADES, PLEASE. I JUST BOUGHT THEM.
FINE. BE THAT WAY.
OGUN-- TAKE THE ISOHELIX.
WHAT'S AN ISOHELIX?
NGHH! GRHHH! URK!
COME ON, MAN, IT'S JUST A Q-TIP.

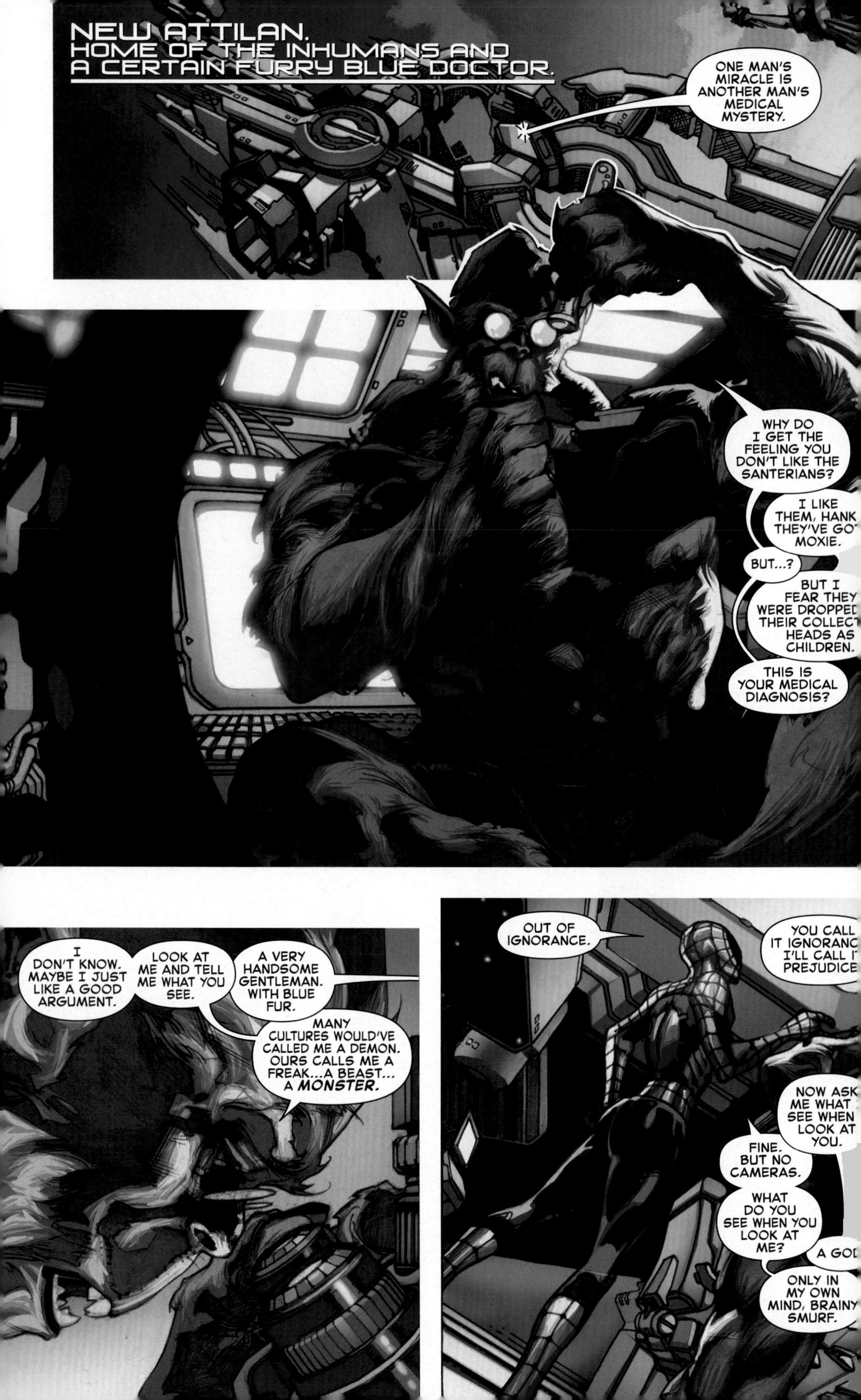
NEW ATTILAN.
HOME OF THE INHUMANS AND A CERTAIN FURRY BLUE DOCTOR.
ONE MAN'S MIRACLE IS ANOTHER MAN'S MEDICAL MYSTERY.
WHY DO I GET THE FEELING YOU DON'T LIKE THE SANTERIANS?
I LIKE THEM, HANK THEY'VE GO MOXIE.
BUT...?
BUT I FEAR THEY WERE DROPPE THEIR COLLEC HEADS AS CHILDREN.
THIS IS YOUR MEDICAL DIAGNOSIS?
I DON'T KNOW. MAYBE I JUST LIKE A GOOD ARGUMENT.
LOOK AT ME AND TELL ME WHAT YOU SEE.
A VERY HANDSOME GENTLEMAN. WITH BLUE FUR.
MANY CULTURES WOULD'VE CALLED ME A DEMON. OURS CALLS ME A FREAK...A BEAST... A MONSTER.
OUT OF IGNORANCE.
YOU CALL IT IGNORANC I'LL CALL I PREJUDICE
NOW ASK ME WHAT SEE WHEN LOOK AT YOU.
FINE. BUT NO CAMERAS.
WHAT DO YOU SEE WHEN YOU LOOK AT ME?
A GO
ONLY IN MY OWN MIND, BRAINY SMURF.

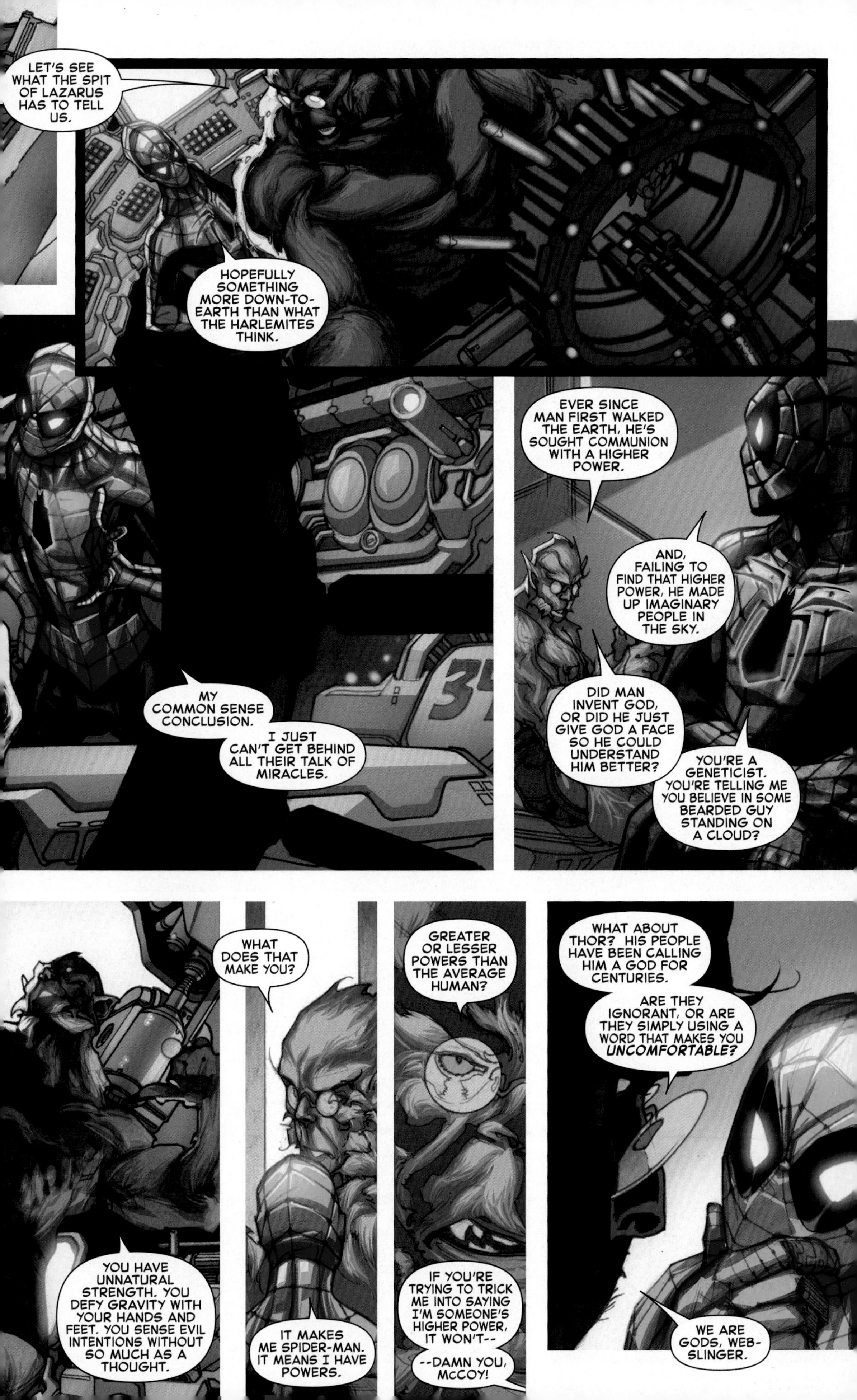
LET'S SEE WHAT THE SPIT OF LAZARUS HAS TO TELL US.
HOPEFULLY SOMETHING MORE DOWN-TO-EARTH THAN WHAT THE HARLEMITES THINK.
MY COMMON SENSE CONCLUSION.
I JUST CAN'T GET BEHIND ALL THEIR TALK OF MIRACLES.
EVER SINCE MAN FIRST WALKED THE EARTH, HE'S SOUGHT COMMUNION WITH A HIGHER POWER.
AND, FAILING TO FIND THAT HIGHER POWER, HE MADE UP IMAGINARY PEOPLE IN THE SKY.
DID MAN INVENT GOD, OR DID HE JUST GIVE GOD A FACE SO HE COULD UNDERSTAND HIM BETTER?
YOU'RE A GENETICIST. YOU'RE TELLING ME YOU BELIEVE IN SOME BEARDED GUY STANDING ON A CLOUD?
YOU HAVE UNNATURAL STRENGTH. YOU DEFY GRAVITY WITH YOUR HANDS AND FEET. YOU SENSE EVIL INTENTIONS WITHOUT SO MUCH AS A THOUGHT.
WHAT DOES THAT MAKE YOU?
IT MAKES ME SPIDER-MAN. IT MEANS I HAVE POWERS.
GREATER OR LESSER POWERS THAN THE AVERAGE HUMAN?
IF YOU'RE TRYING TO TRICK ME INTO SAYING I'M SOMEONE'S HIGHER POWER, IT WON'T--
--DAMN YOU, McCOY!
WHAT ABOUT THOR? HIS PEOPLE HAVE BEEN CALLING HIM A GOD FOR CENTURIES.
ARE THEY IGNORANT, OR ARE THEY SIMPLY USING A WORD THAT MAKES YOU *UNCOMFORTABLE?*
WE ARE GODS, WEB-SLINGER.

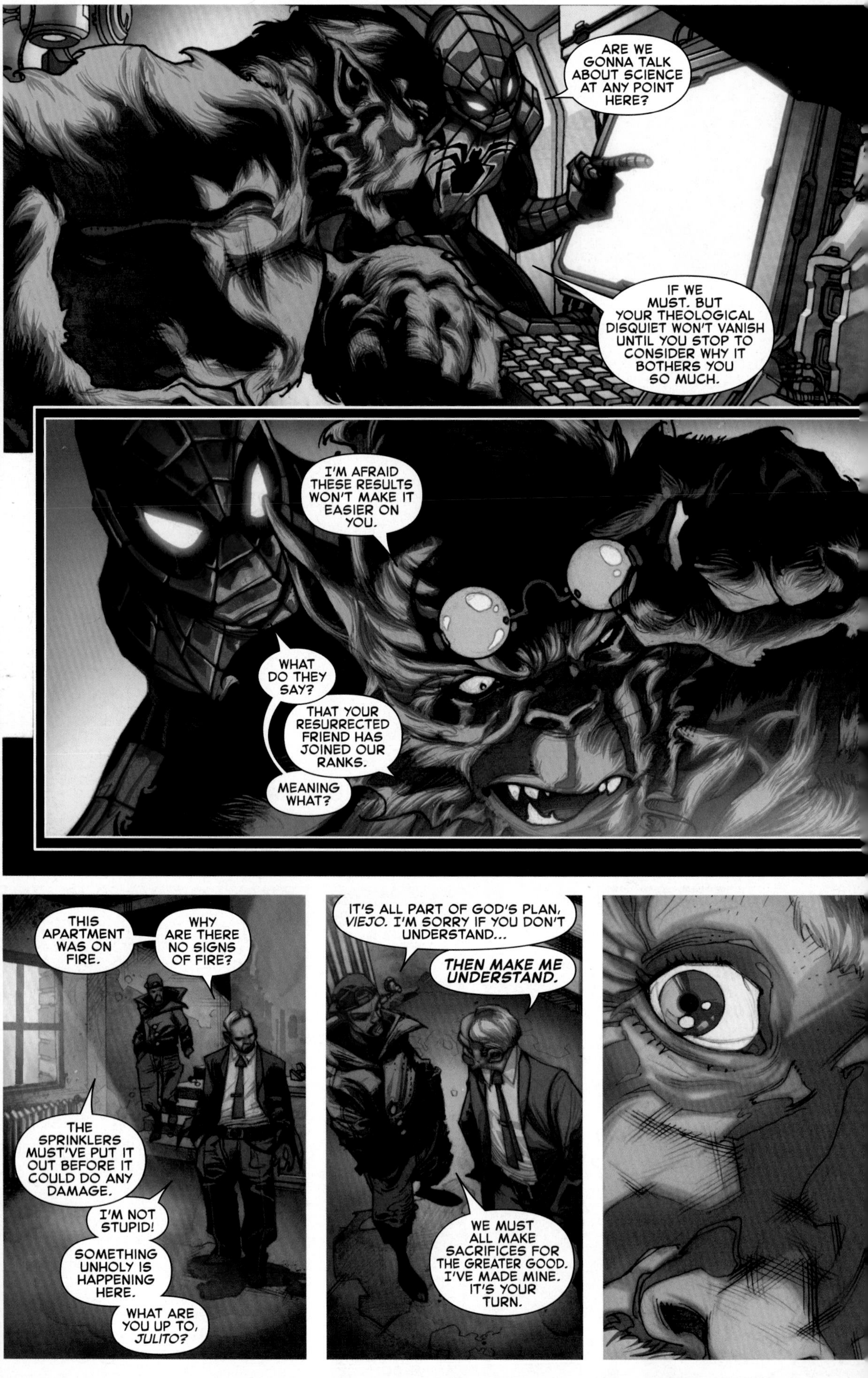
ARE WE GONNA TALK ABOUT SCIENCE AT ANY POINT HERE?
IF WE MUST. BUT YOUR THEOLOGICAL DISQUIET WON'T VANISH UNTIL YOU STOP TO CONSIDER WHY IT BOTHERS YOU SO MUCH.
I'M AFRAID THESE RESULTS WON'T MAKE IT EASIER ON YOU.
WHAT DO THEY SAY?
THAT YOUR RESURRECTED FRIEND HAS JOINED OUR RANKS.
MEANING WHAT?
THIS APARTMENT WAS ON FIRE.
WHY ARE THERE NO SIGNS OF FIRE?
THE SPRINKLERS MUST'VE PUT IT OUT BEFORE IT COULD DO ANY DAMAGE.
I'M NOT STUPID!
SOMETHING UNHOLY IS HAPPENING HERE.
WHAT ARE YOU UP TO, *JULITO?*
IT'S ALL PART OF GOD'S PLAN, *VIEJO.* I'M SORRY IF YOU DON'T UNDERSTAND...
THEN MAKE ME UNDERSTAND.
WE MUST ALL MAKE SACRIFICES FOR THE GREATER GOOD. I'VE MADE MINE. IT'S YOUR TURN.

I'M NOT SAYING HE'S A GOD...

BUT HE'S NO LONGER HUMAN.

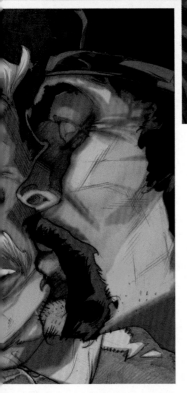

I LOVE YOU, VIEJO.

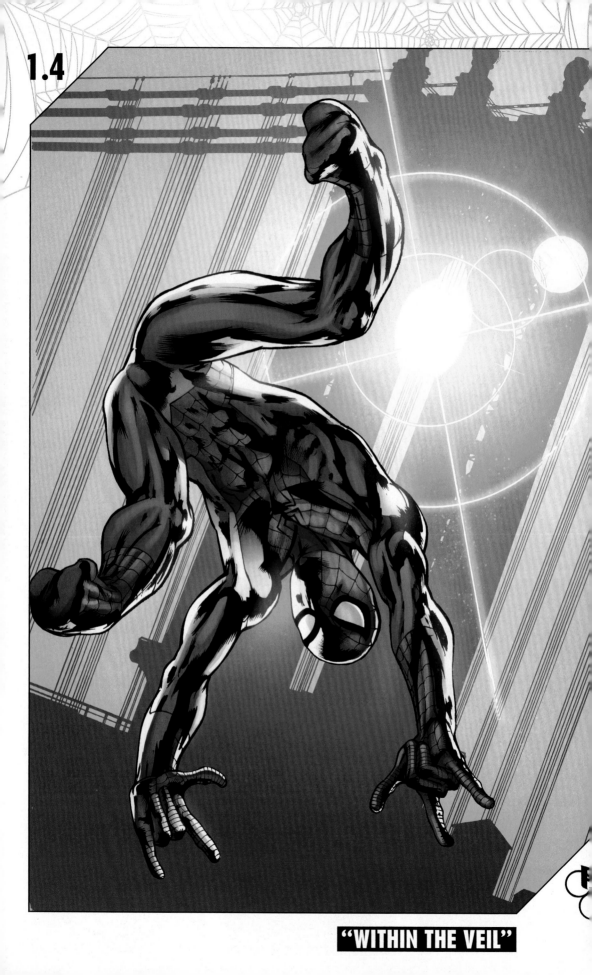

"WITHIN THE VEIL"

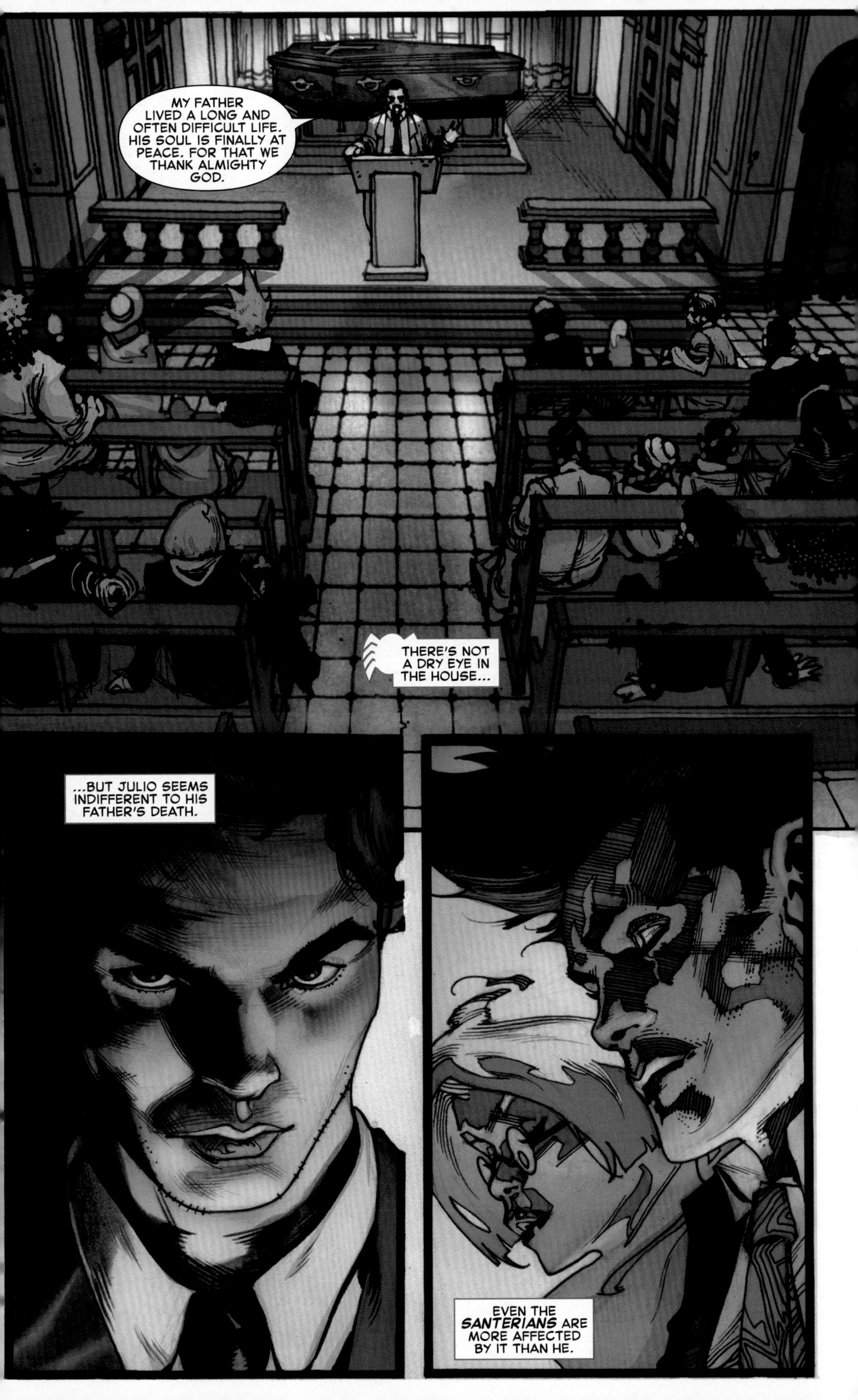
MY FATHER LIVED A LONG AND OFTEN DIFFICULT LIFE. HIS SOUL IS FINALLY AT PEACE. FOR THAT WE THANK ALMIGHTY GOD.
THERE'S NOT A DRY EYE IN THE HOUSE...
...BUT JULIO SEEMS INDIFFERENT TO HIS FATHER'S DEATH.
EVEN THE SANTERIANS ARE MORE AFFECTED BY IT THAN HE.

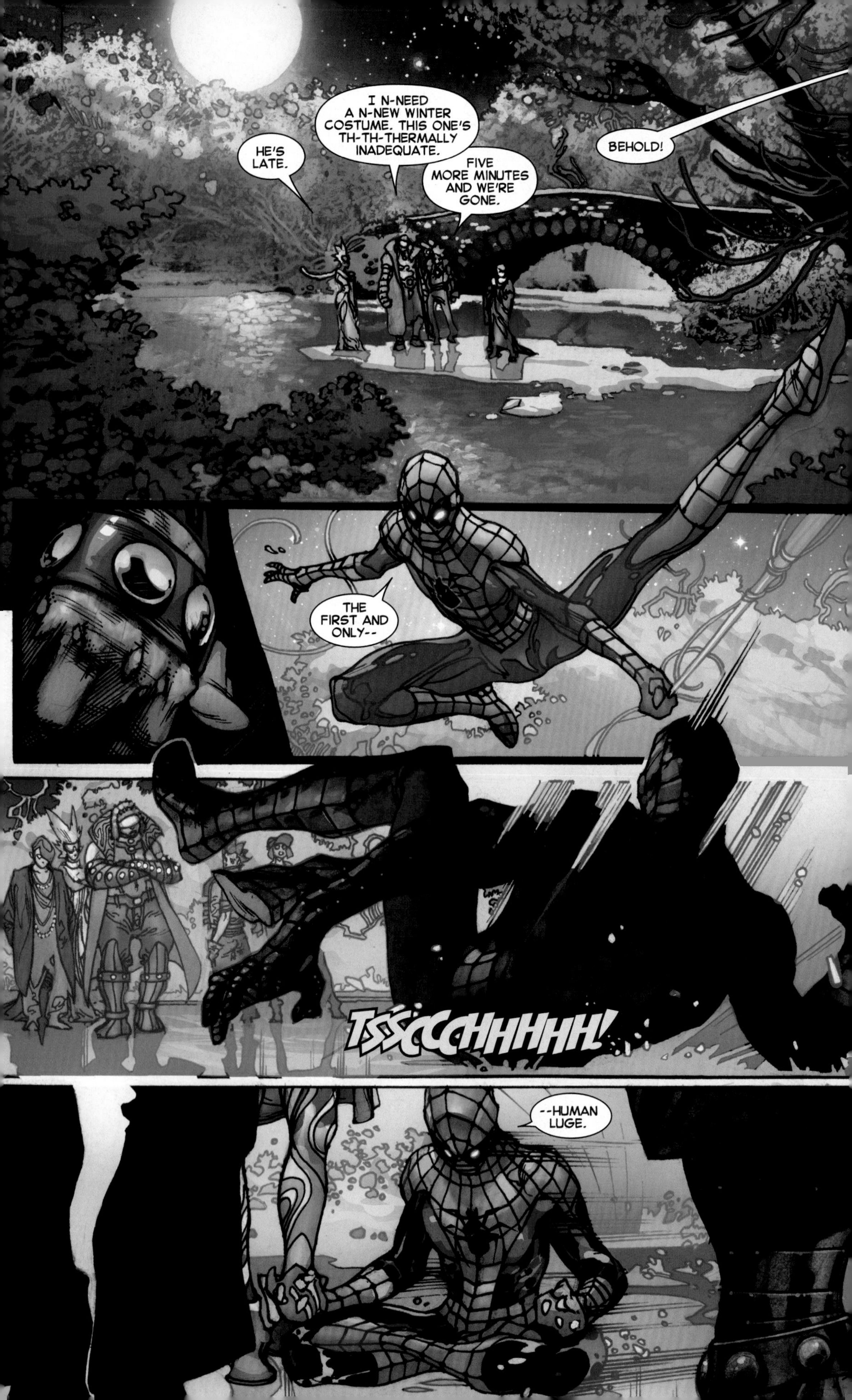
HE'S LATE.
I N-NEED A N-NEW WINTER COSTUME. THIS ONE'S TH-TH-THERMALLY INADEQUATE.
FIVE MORE MINUTES AND WE'RE GONE.
BEHOLD!
THE FIRST AND ONLY--
TSSCCCHHHHH!
--HUMAN LUGE.

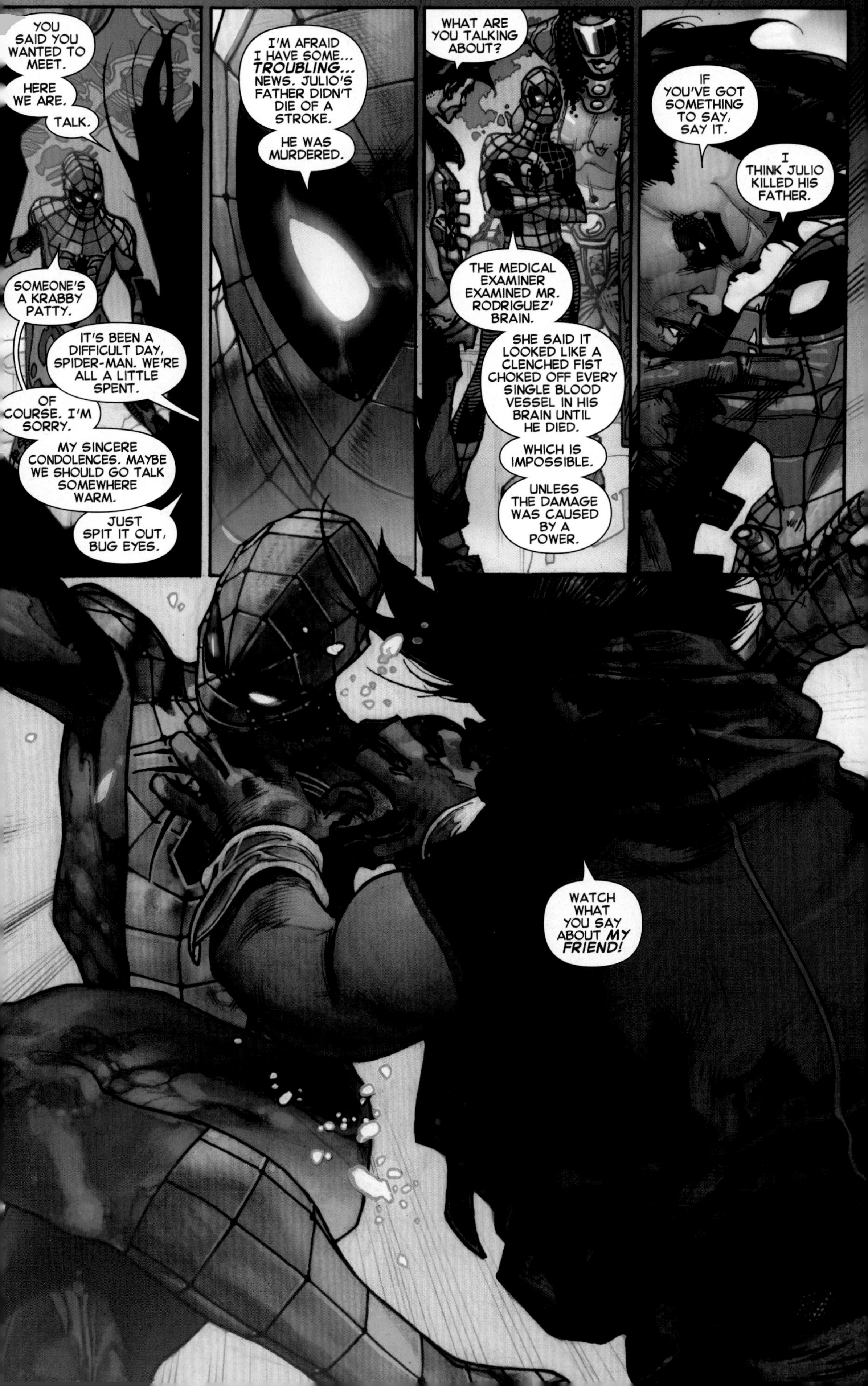

YOU SAID YOU WANTED TO MEET.
HERE WE ARE.
TALK.
SOMEONE'S A KRABBY PATTY.
IT'S BEEN A DIFFICULT DAY, SPIDER-MAN. WE'RE ALL A LITTLE SPENT.
OF COURSE. I'M SORRY.
MY SINCERE CONDOLENCES. MAYBE WE SHOULD GO TALK SOMEWHERE WARM.
JUST SPIT IT OUT, BUG EYES.
I'M AFRAID I HAVE SOME... ***TROUBLING...*** NEWS. JULIO'S FATHER DIDN'T DIE OF A STROKE.
HE WAS MURDERED.
WHAT ARE YOU TALKING ABOUT?
THE MEDICAL EXAMINER EXAMINED MR. RODRIGUEZ' BRAIN.
SHE SAID IT LOOKED LIKE A CLENCHED FIST CHOKED OFF EVERY SINGLE BLOOD VESSEL IN HIS BRAIN UNTIL HE DIED.
WHICH IS IMPOSSIBLE.
UNLESS THE DAMAGE WAS CAUSED BY A POWER.
IF YOU'VE GOT SOMETHING TO SAY, SAY IT.
I THINK JULIO KILLED HIS FATHER.
WATCH WHAT YOU SAY ABOUT ***MY FRIEND!***

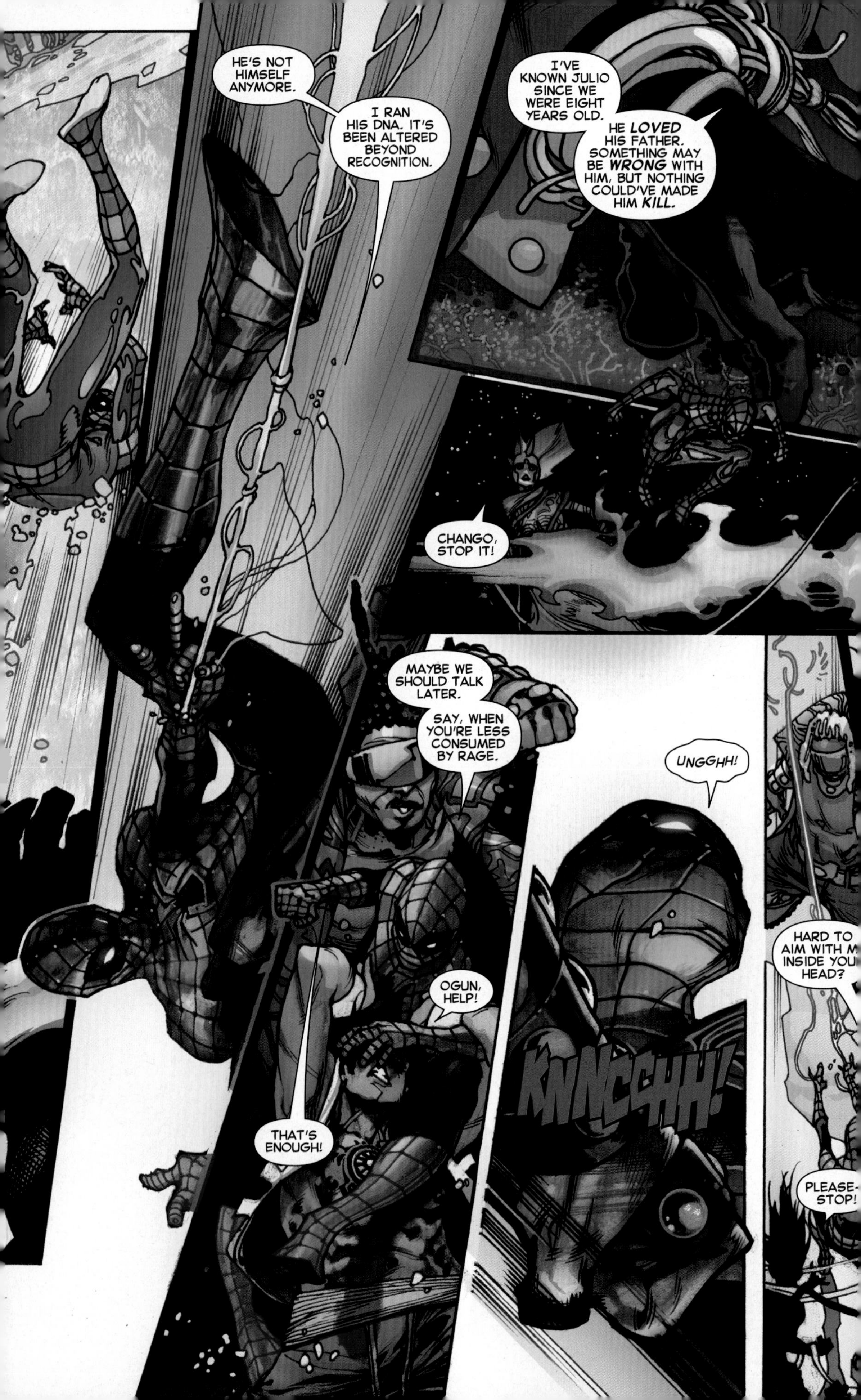
HE'S NOT HIMSELF ANYMORE.
I RAN HIS DNA. IT'S BEEN ALTERED BEYOND RECOGNITION.
I'VE KNOWN JULIO SINCE WE WERE EIGHT YEARS OLD.
HE *LOVED* HIS FATHER. SOMETHING MAY BE *WRONG* WITH HIM, BUT NOTHING COULD'VE MADE HIM *KILL.*
CHANGO, STOP IT!
MAYBE WE SHOULD TALK LATER.
SAY, WHEN YOU'RE LESS CONSUMED BY RAGE.
OGUN, HELP!
THAT'S ENOUGH!
UNGGHH!
KNNCCHH!
PLEASE-STOP!

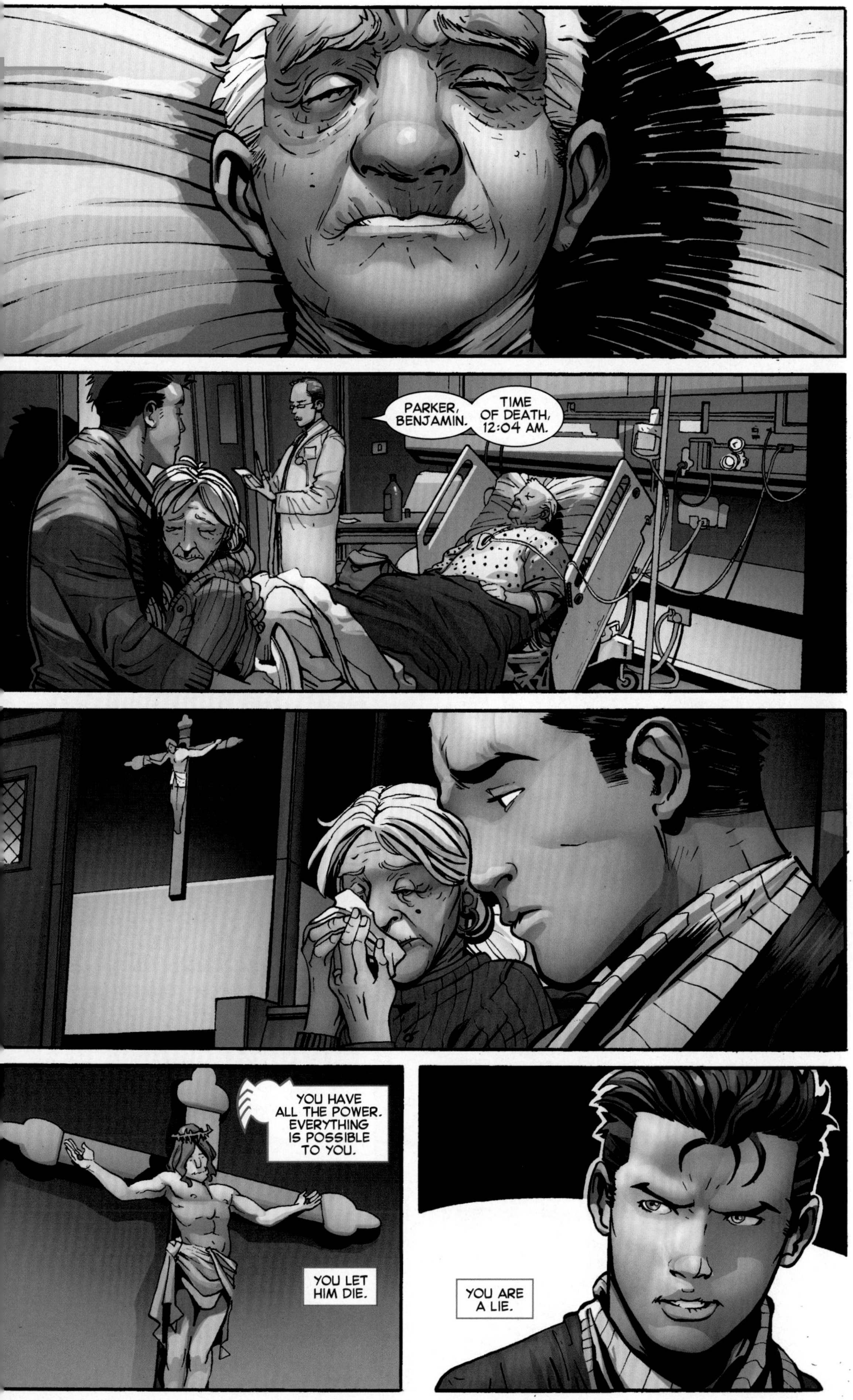
PARKER, BENJAMIN.
TIME OF DEATH, 12:04 AM.
YOU HAVE ALL THE POWER. EVERYTHING IS POSSIBLE TO YOU.
YOU LET HIM DIE.
YOU ARE A LIE.

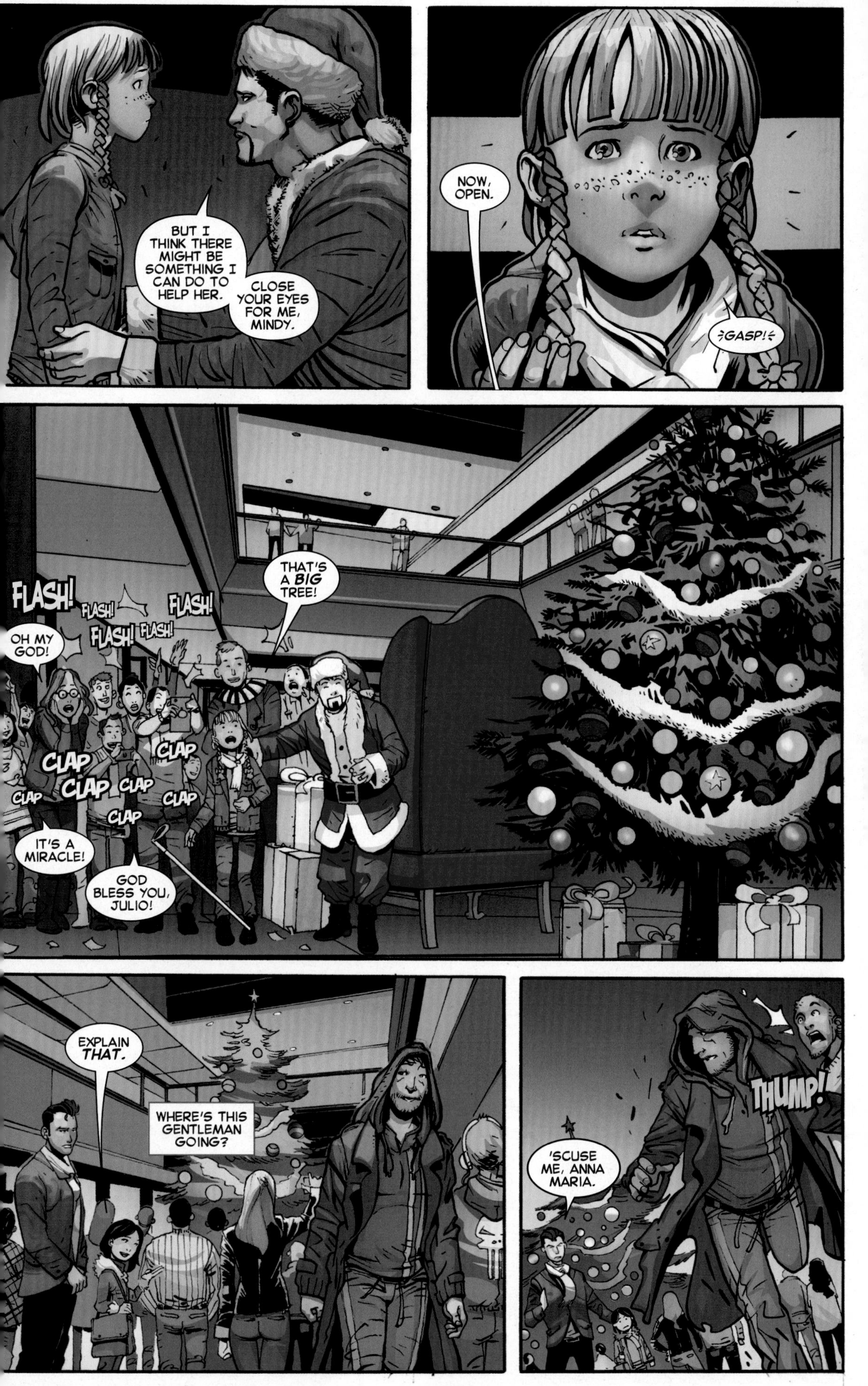
BUT I THINK THERE MIGHT BE SOMETHING I CAN DO TO HELP HER.
CLOSE YOUR EYES FOR ME, MINDY.
NOW, OPEN.
GASP!
FLASH!
FLASH!
FLASH!
FLASH!
FLASH!
THAT'S A BIG TREE!
OH MY GOD!
CLAP
CLAP
CLAP
CLAP
CLAP
CLAP
CLAP
IT'S A MIRACLE!
GOD BLESS YOU, JULIO!
EXPLAIN THAT.
WHERE'S THIS GENTLEMAN GOING?
THUMP!
'SCUSE ME, ANNA MARIA.

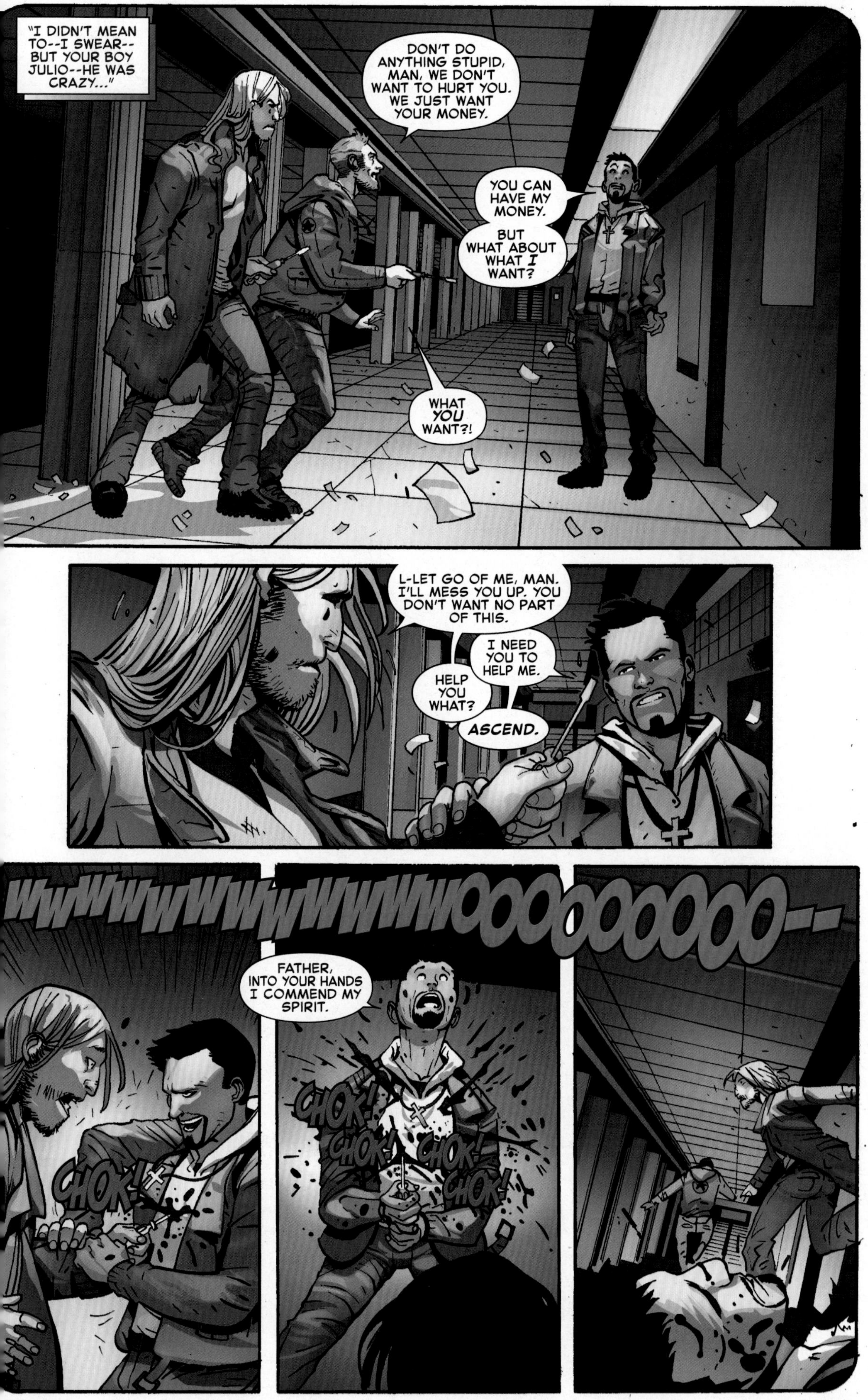
"I DIDN'T MEAN TO--I SWEAR--BUT YOUR BOY JULIO--HE WAS CRAZY..."
DON'T DO ANYTHING STUPID, MAN, WE DON'T WANT TO HURT YOU. WE JUST WANT YOUR MONEY.
YOU CAN HAVE MY MONEY.
BUT WHAT ABOUT WHAT *I* WANT?
WHAT *YOU* WANT?!
L-LET GO OF ME, MAN. I'LL MESS YOU UP. YOU DON'T WANT NO PART OF THIS.
I NEED YOU TO HELP ME.
HELP YOU WHAT?
ASCEND.
WWWWWWWWWWWWWOOOOOOOOOO--
CHOK!
FATHER, INTO YOUR HANDS I COMMEND MY SPIRIT.
CHOK! CHOK! CHOK! CHOK!

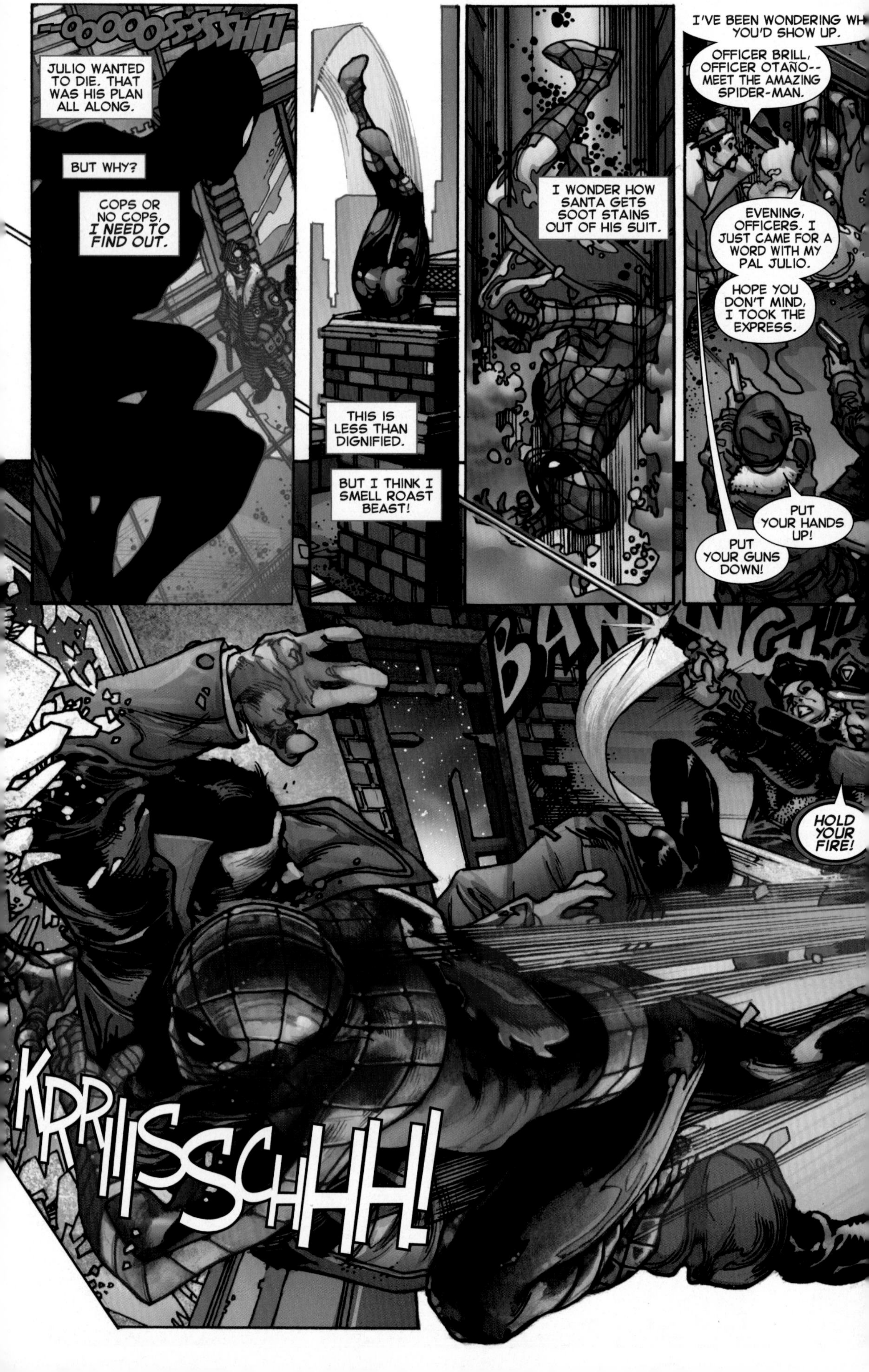
-OOOOOSSSSHH
JULIO WANTED TO DIE. THAT WAS HIS PLAN ALL ALONG.
BUT WHY?
COPS OR NO COPS, *I NEED TO FIND OUT.*
THIS IS LESS THAN DIGNIFIED.
BUT I THINK I SMELL ROAST BEAST!
I WONDER HOW SANTA GETS SOOT STAINS OUT OF HIS SUIT.
I'VE BEEN WONDERING WH YOU'D SHOW UP.
OFFICER BRILL, OFFICER OTAÑO-- MEET THE AMAZING SPIDER-MAN.
EVENING, OFFICERS. I JUST CAME FOR A WORD WITH MY PAL JULIO.
HOPE YOU DON'T MIND, I TOOK THE EXPRESS.
PUT YOUR HANDS UP!
PUT YOUR GUNS DOWN!
HOLD YOUR FIRE!
KRRIIISSCHHH!

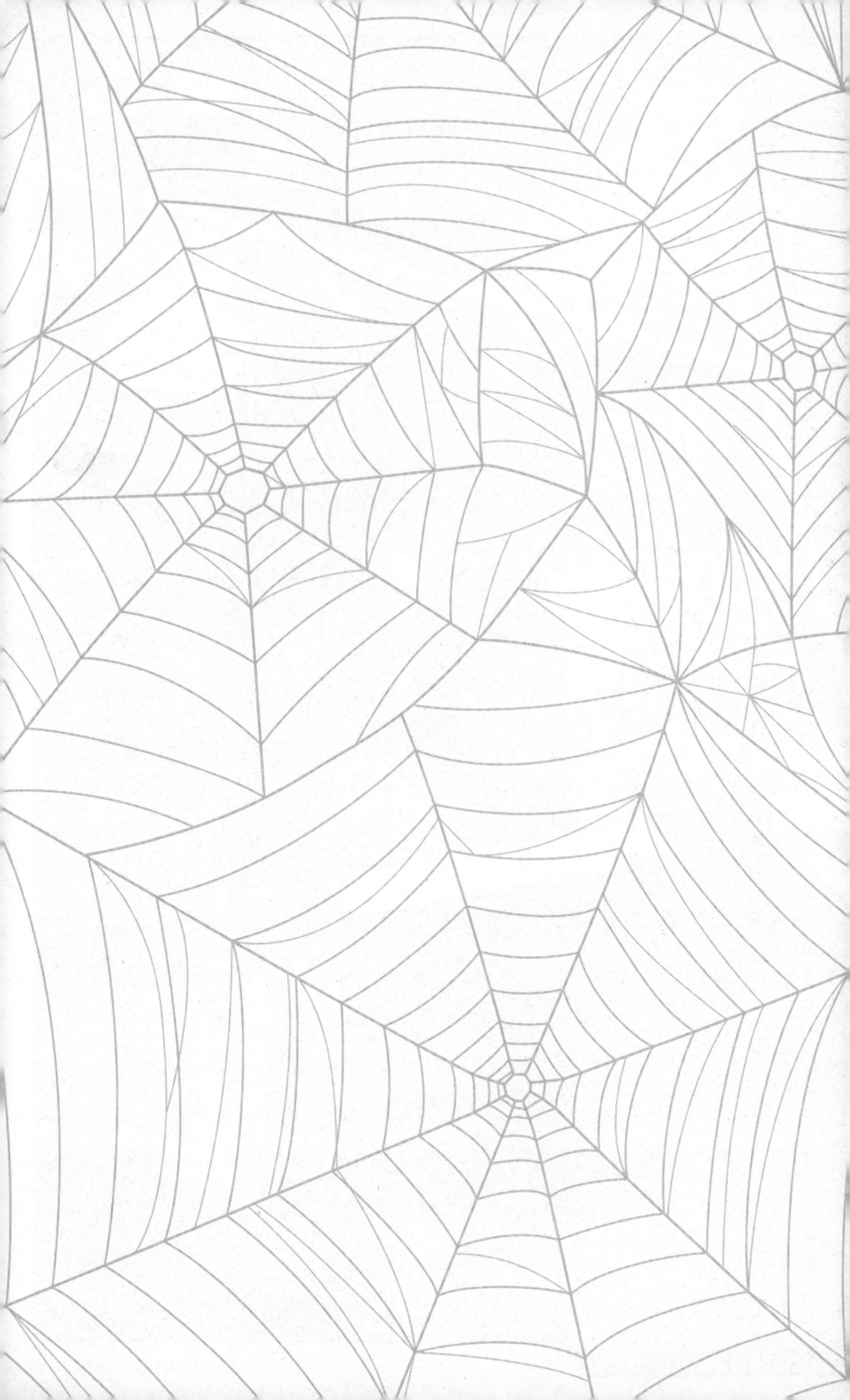

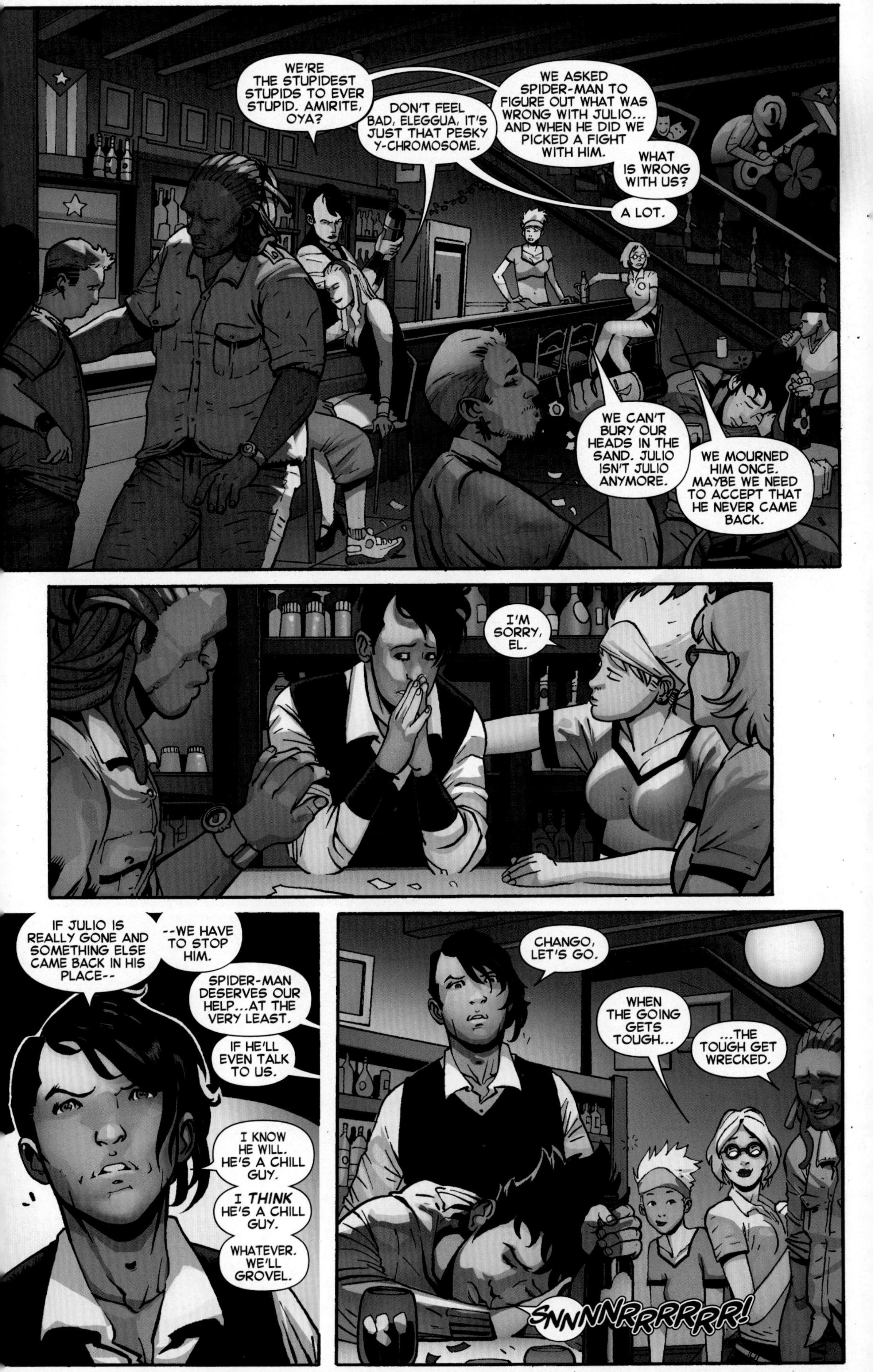

WE'RE THE STUPIDEST STUPIDS TO EVER STUPID. AMIRITE, OYA?
DON'T FEEL BAD, ELEGGUA, IT'S JUST THAT PESKY Y-CHROMOSOME.
WE ASKED SPIDER-MAN TO FIGURE OUT WHAT WAS WRONG WITH JULIO... AND WHEN HE DID WE PICKED A FIGHT WITH HIM.
WHAT IS WRONG WITH US?
A LOT.
WE CAN'T BURY OUR HEADS IN THE SAND. JULIO ISN'T JULIO ANYMORE.
WE MOURNED HIM ONCE. MAYBE WE NEED TO ACCEPT THAT HE NEVER CAME BACK.
I'M SORRY, EL.
IF JULIO IS REALLY GONE AND SOMETHING ELSE CAME BACK IN HIS PLACE--
--WE HAVE TO STOP HIM.
SPIDER-MAN DESERVES OUR HELP...AT THE VERY LEAST.
IF HE'LL EVEN TALK TO US.
I KNOW HE WILL. HE'S A CHILL GUY.
I *THINK* HE'S A CHILL GUY.
WHATEVER. WE'LL GROVEL.
CHANGO, LET'S GO.
WHEN THE GOING GETS TOUGH...
...THE TOUGH GET WRECKED.
SNNNNRRRRRR!

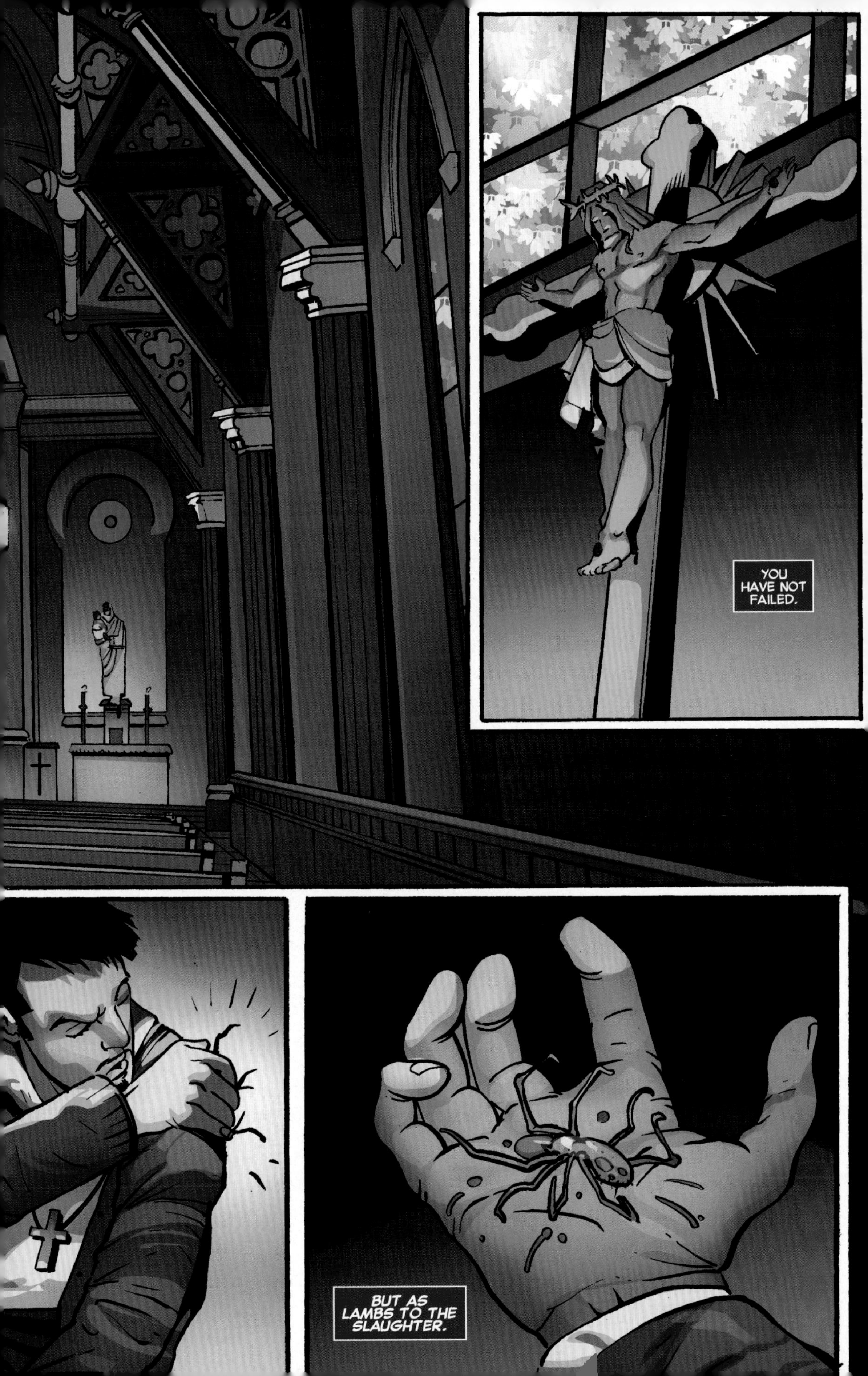
YOU HAVE NOT FAILED.
BUT AS LAMBS TO THE SLAUGHTER.

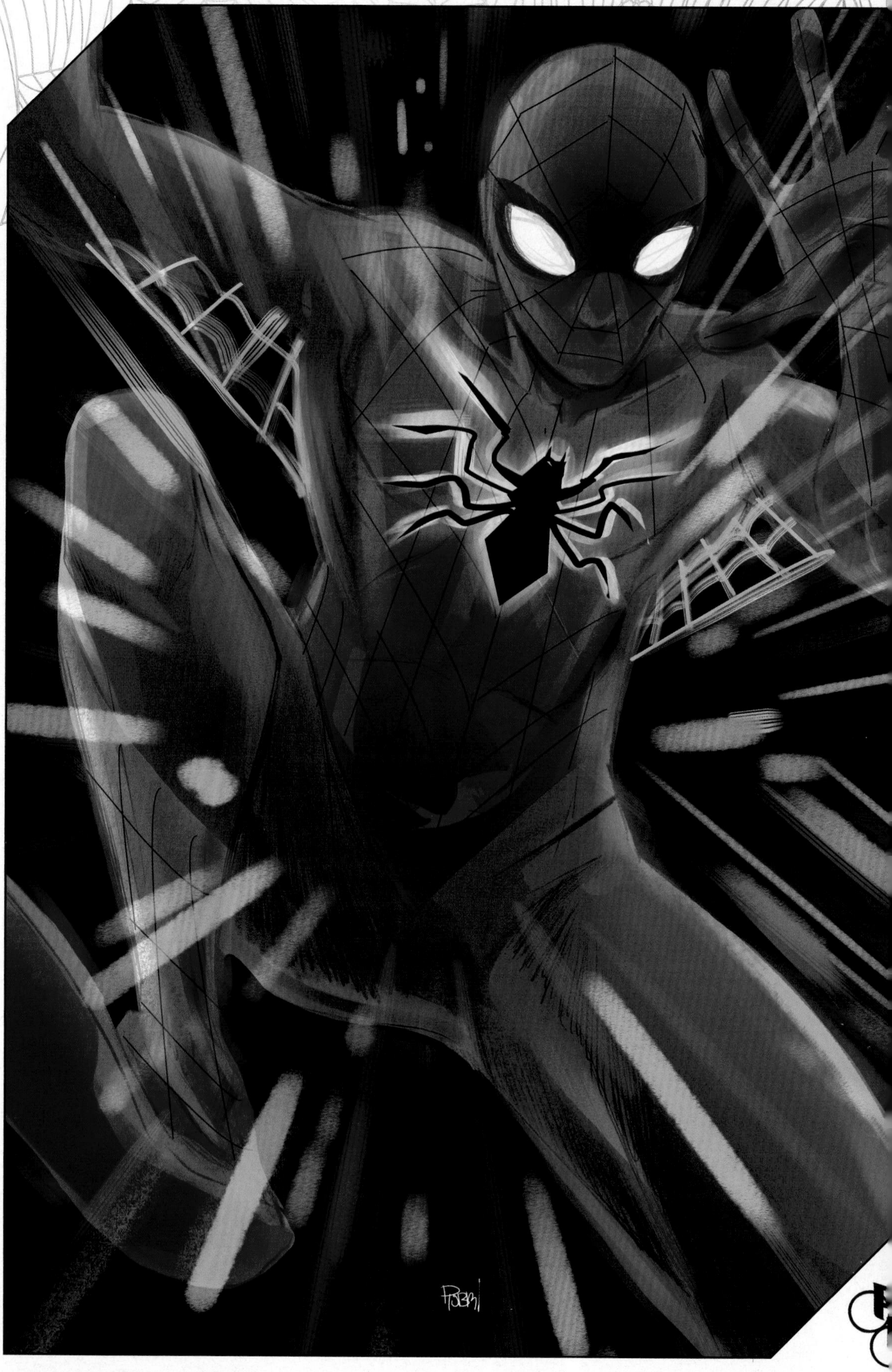

#1.1 VARIANT BY **ROBBI RODRIGUEZ**

1.5

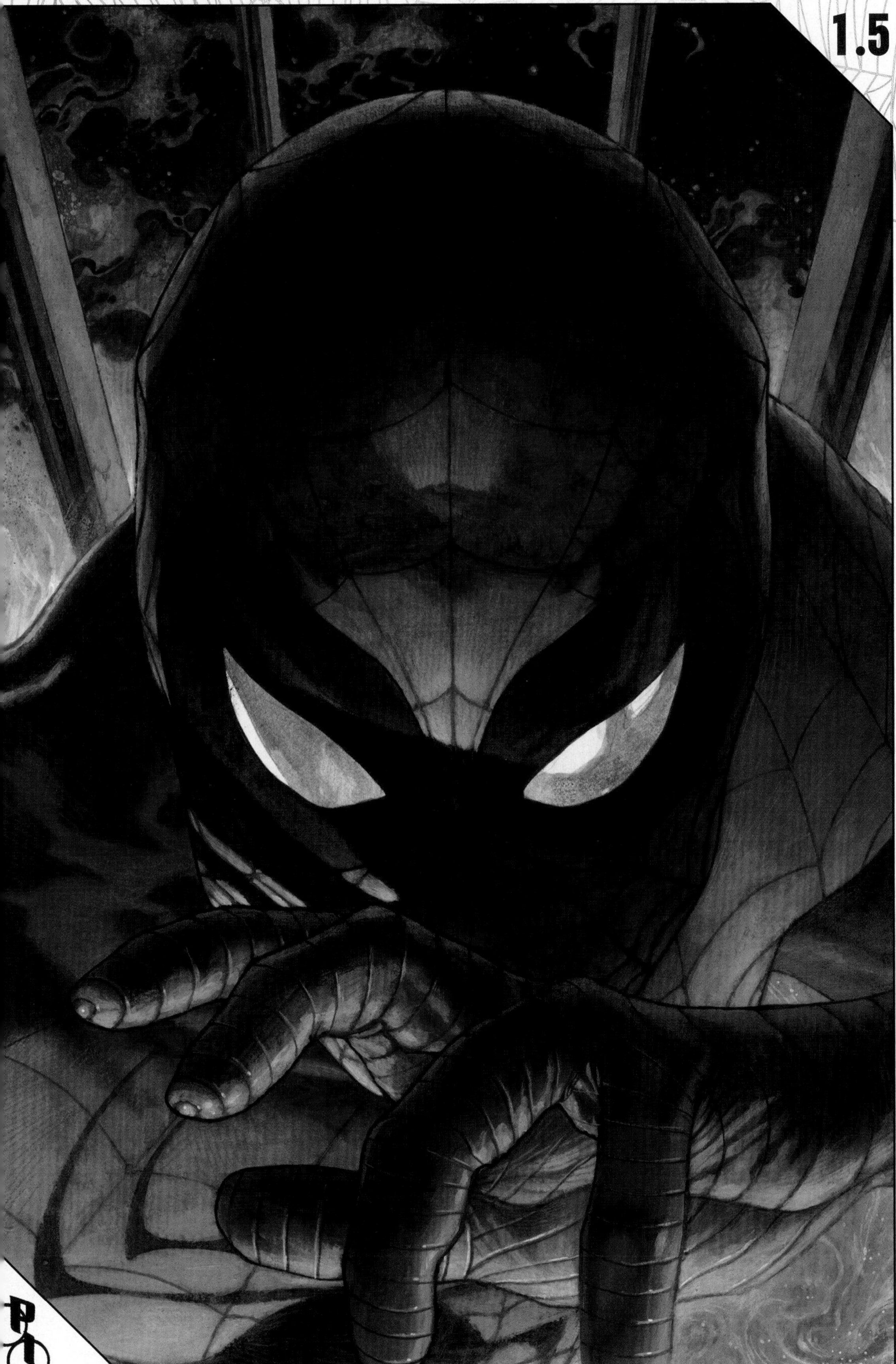

"FLESH AND HEART SHALL FAIL"

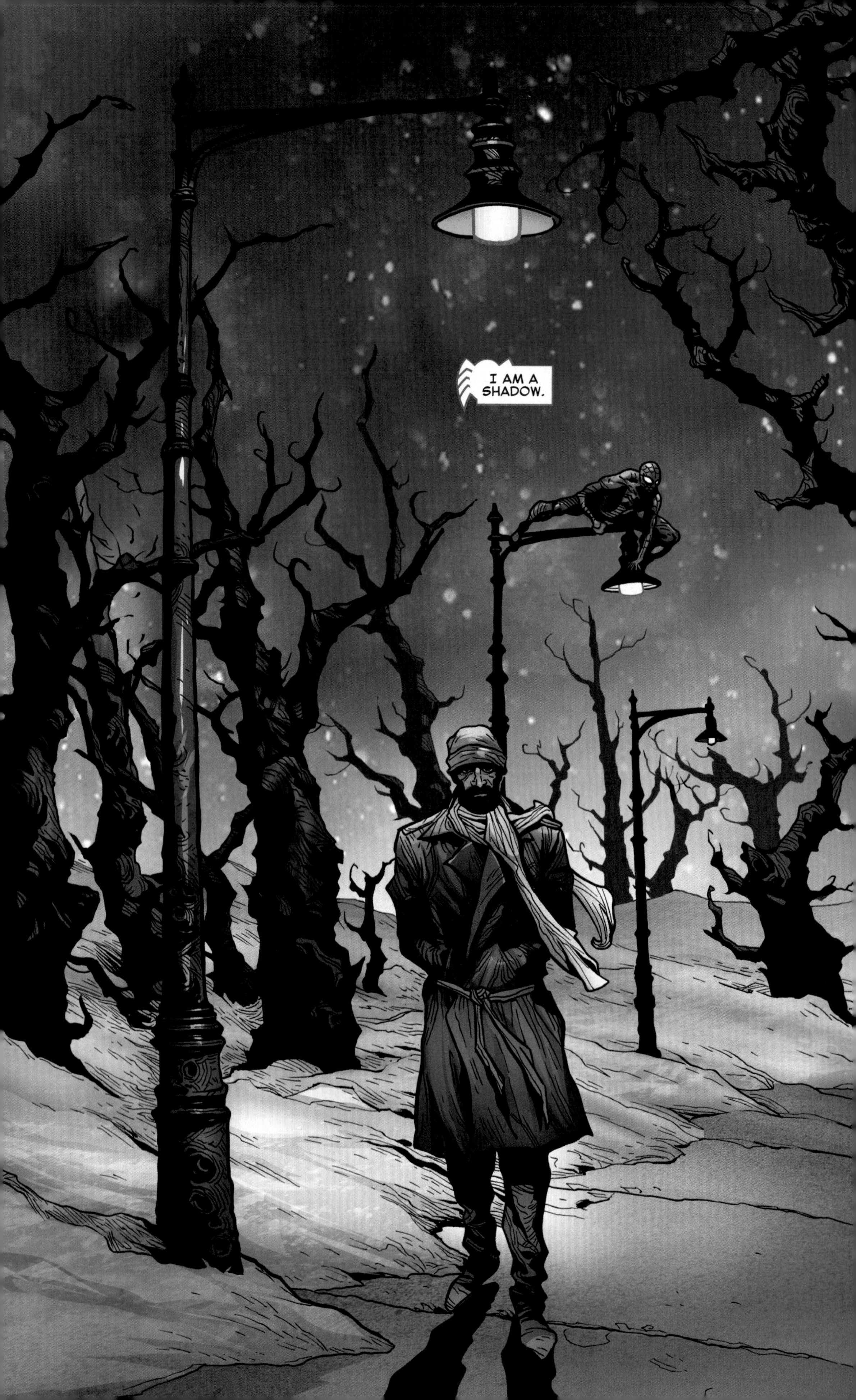
I AM A SHADOW.

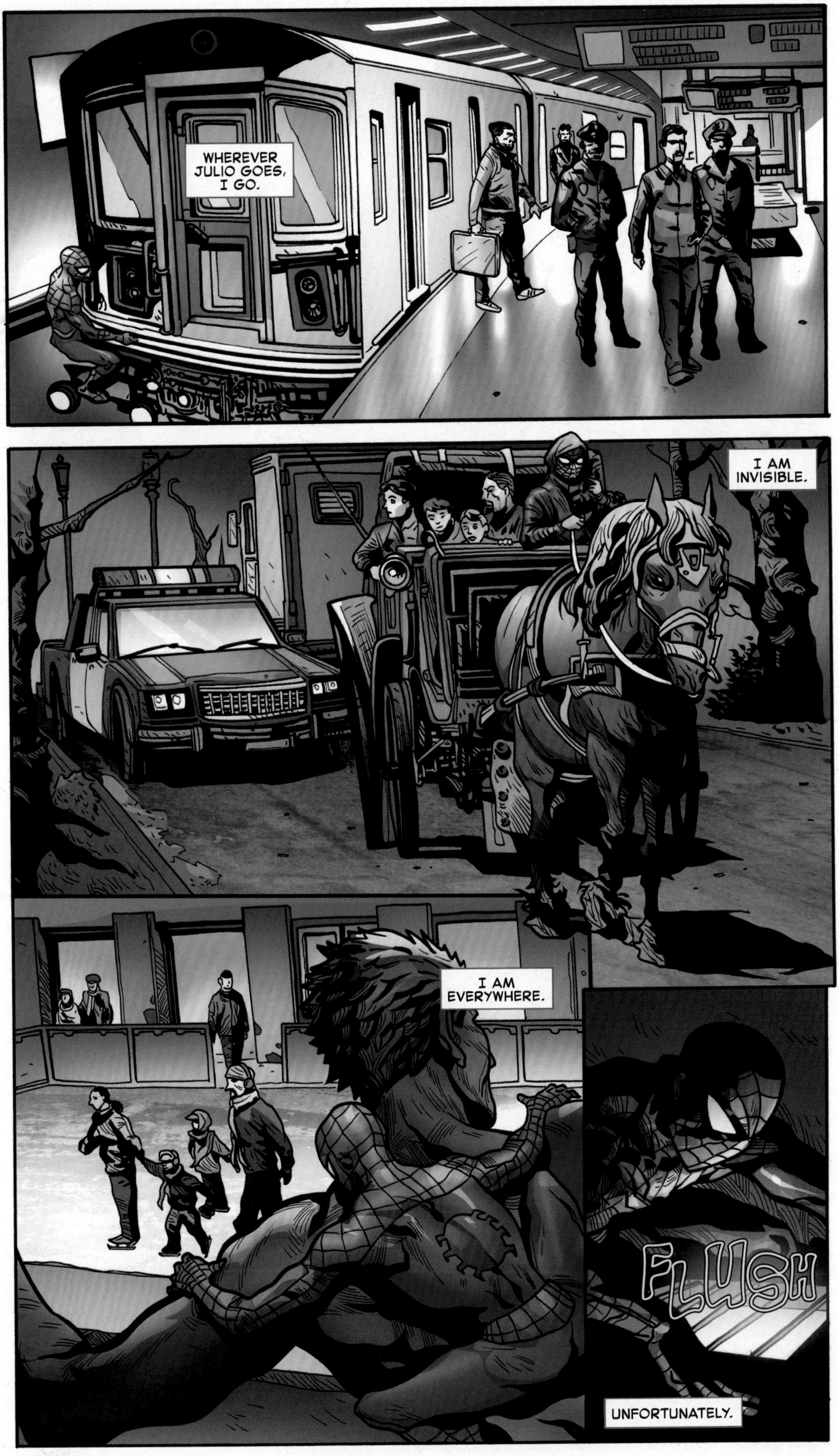
WHEREVER JULIO GOES, I GO.
I AM INVISIBLE.
I AM EVERYWHERE.
FLUSH
UNFORTUNATELY.

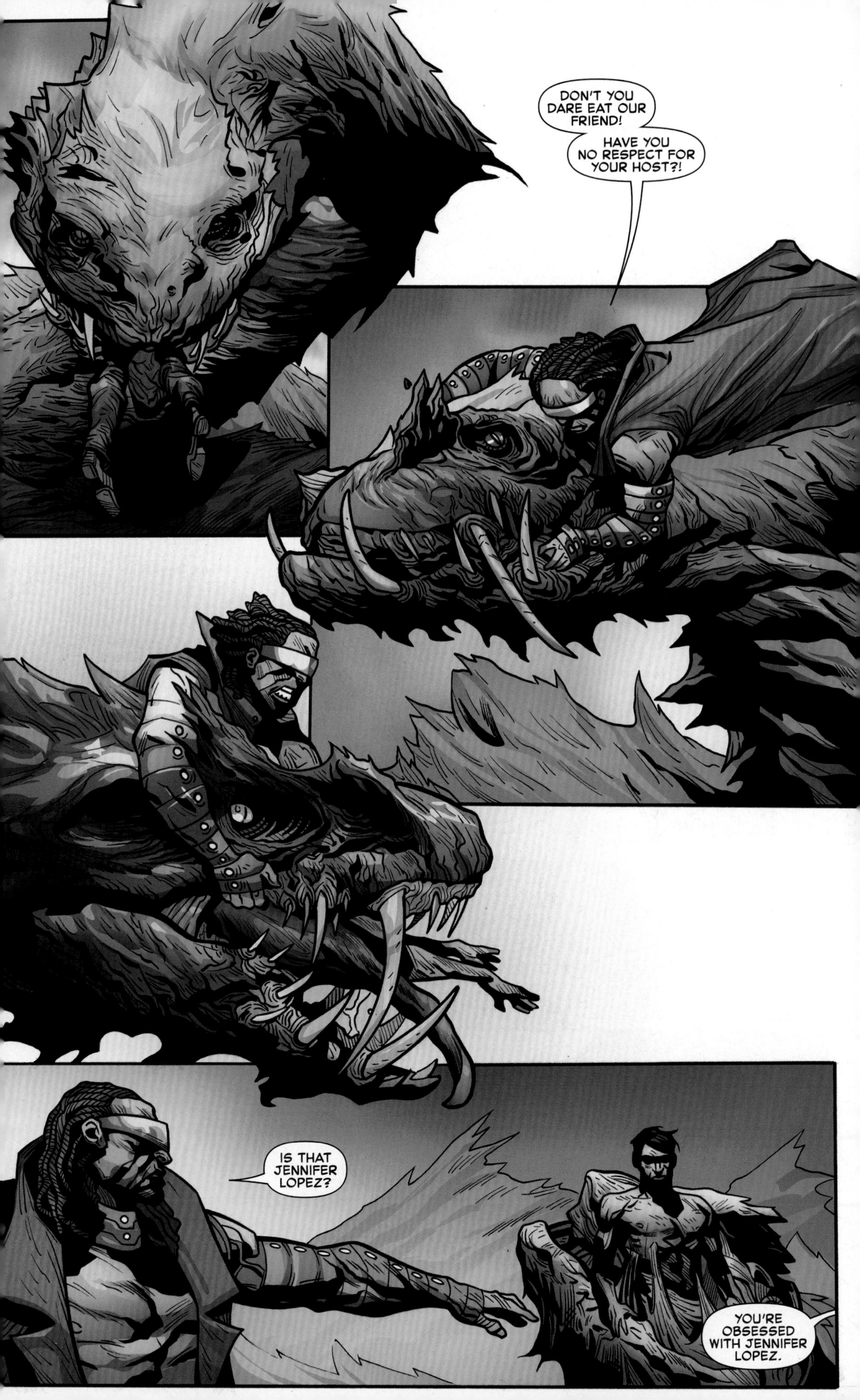
DON'T YOU DARE EAT OUR FRIEND!
HAVE YOU NO RESPECT FOR YOUR HOST?!
IS THAT JENNIFER LOPEZ?
YOU'RE OBSESSED WITH JENNIFER LOPEZ.

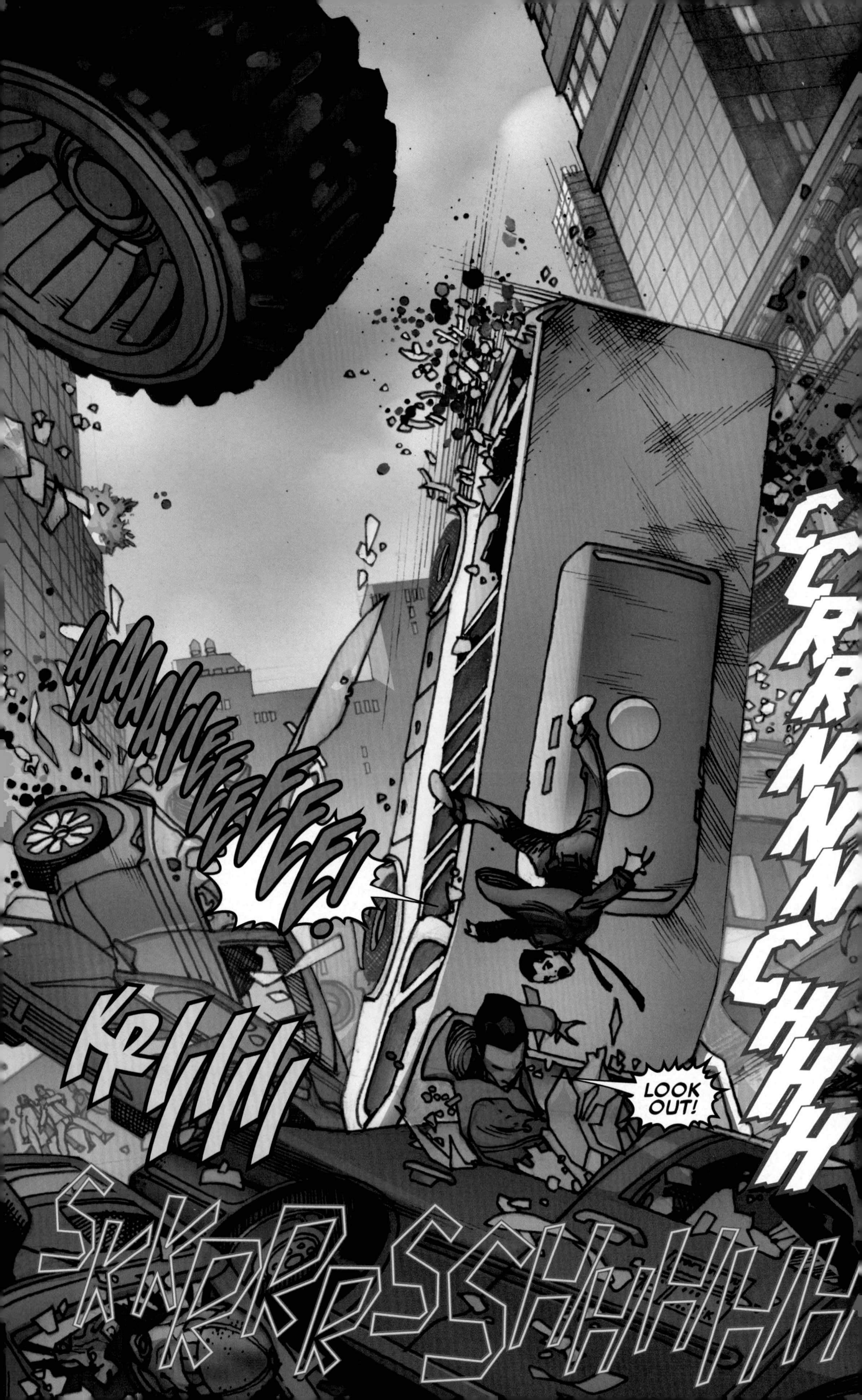
LOOK OUT!

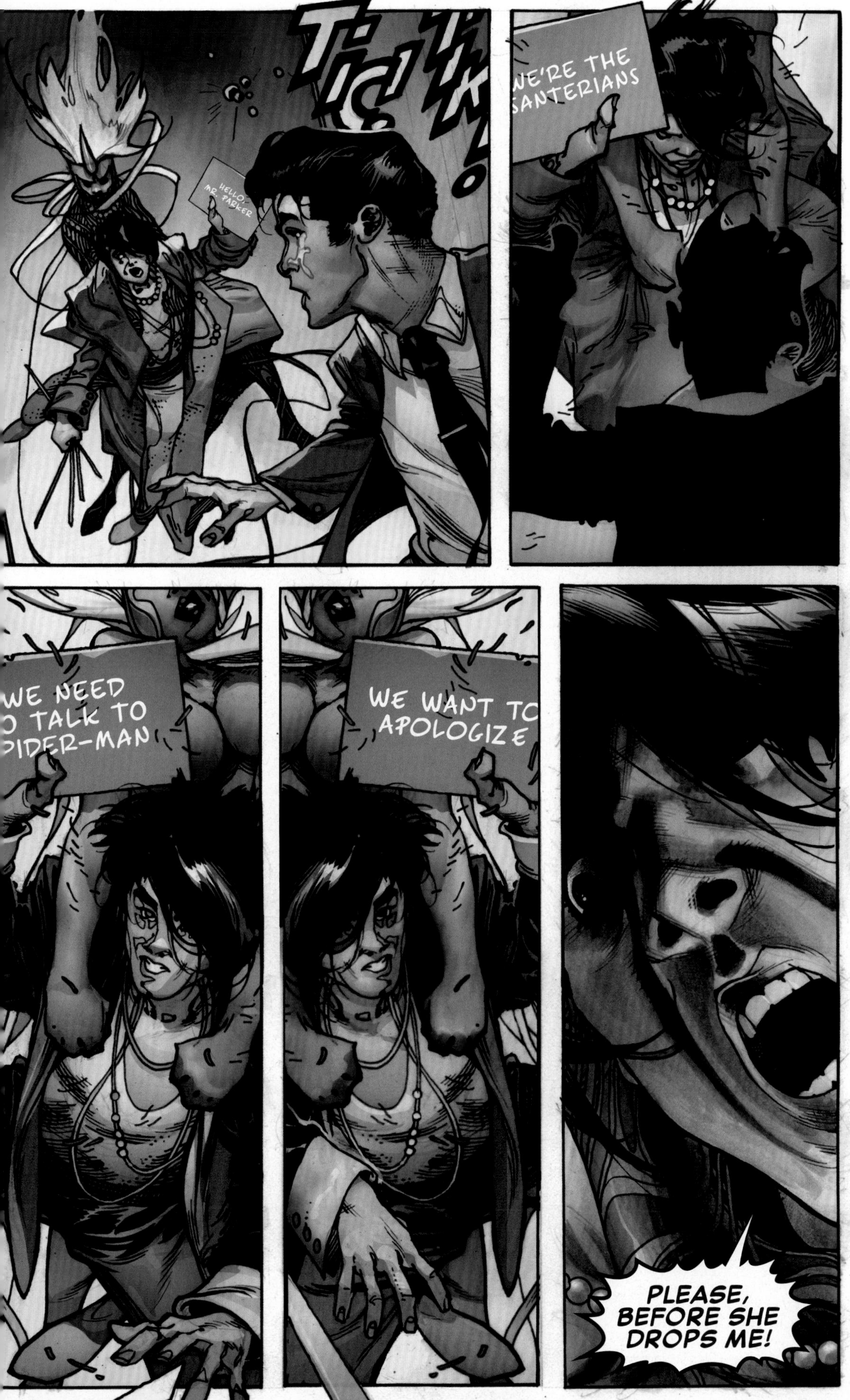
HELLO, MR. PARKER
WE'RE THE SANTERIANS
WE NEED
O TALK TO
PIDER-MAN
WE WANT TO
APOLOGIZE
PLEASE, BEFORE SHE DROPS ME!

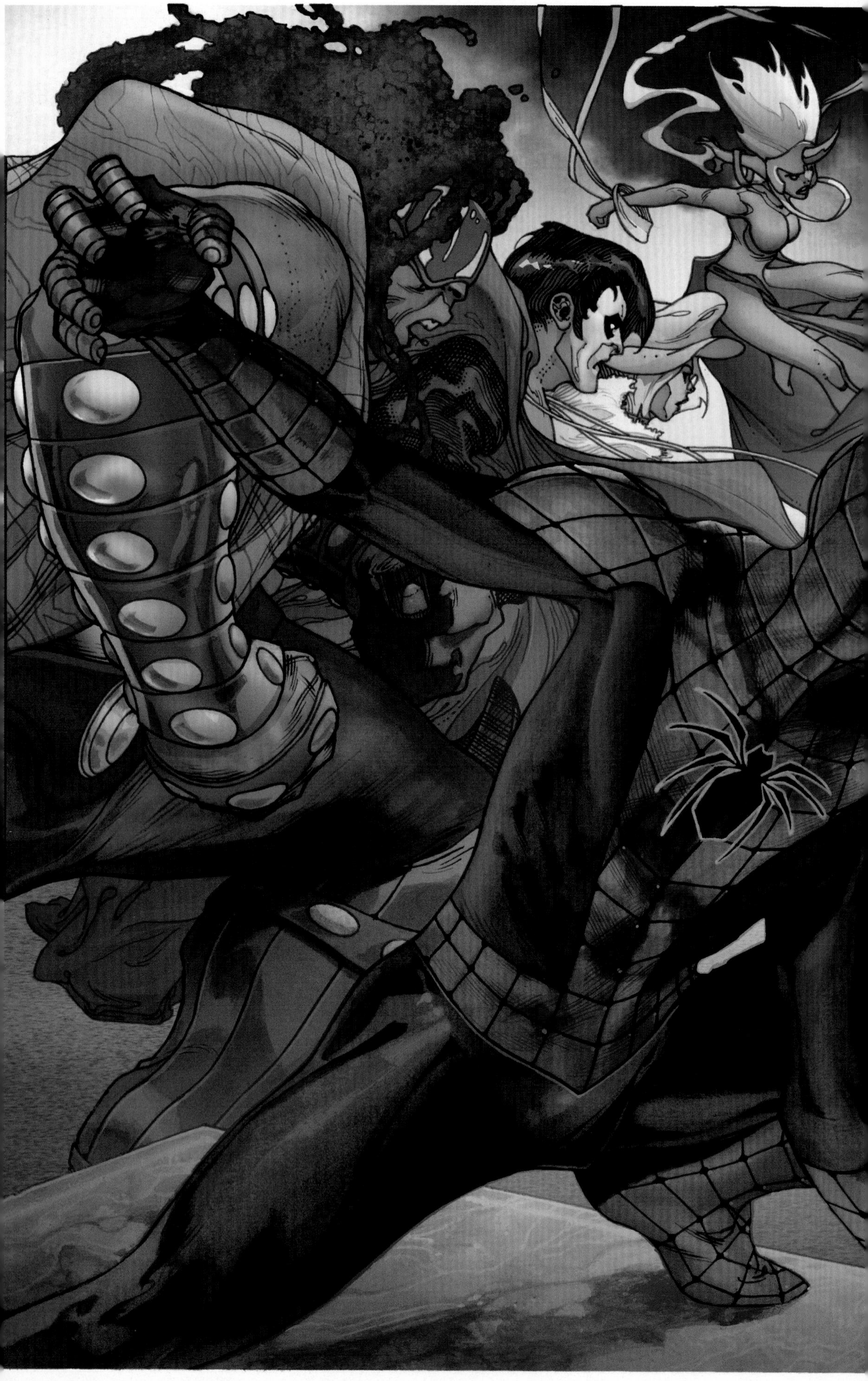

1.6

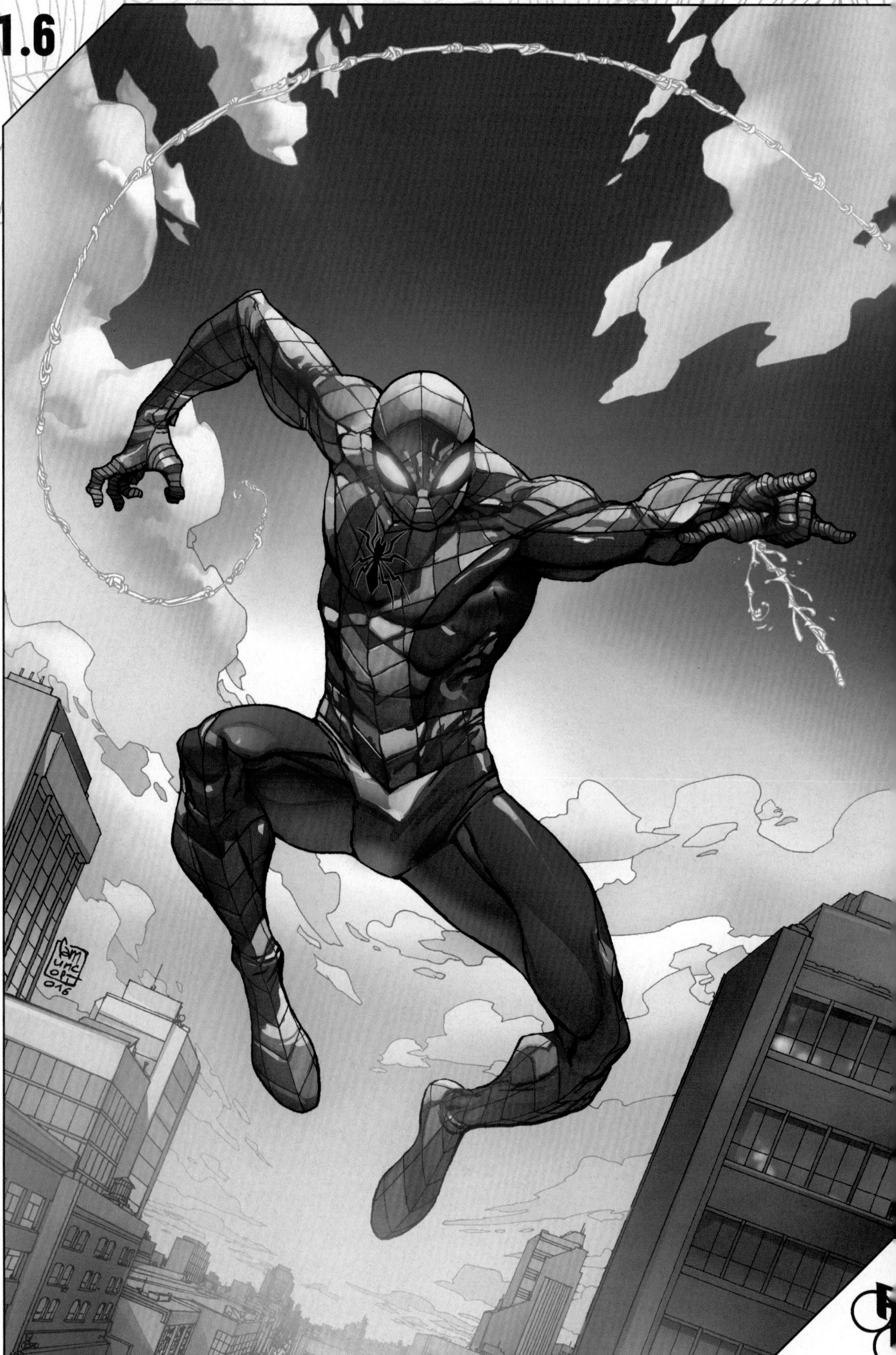

"LEAD ME HOME"

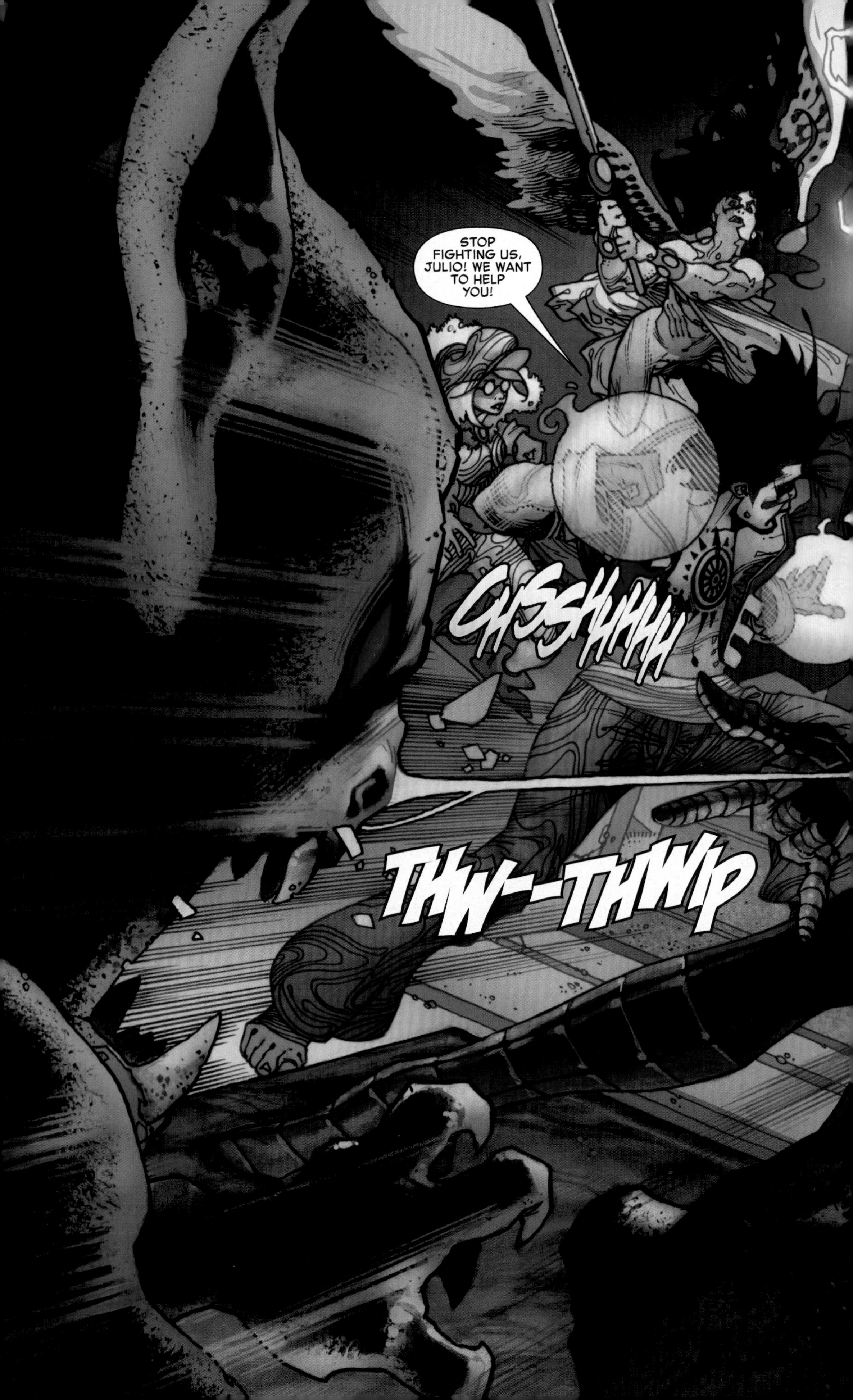
STOP FIGHTING US, JULIO! WE WANT TO HELP YOU!
CHSSHHHH
THW--THWIP

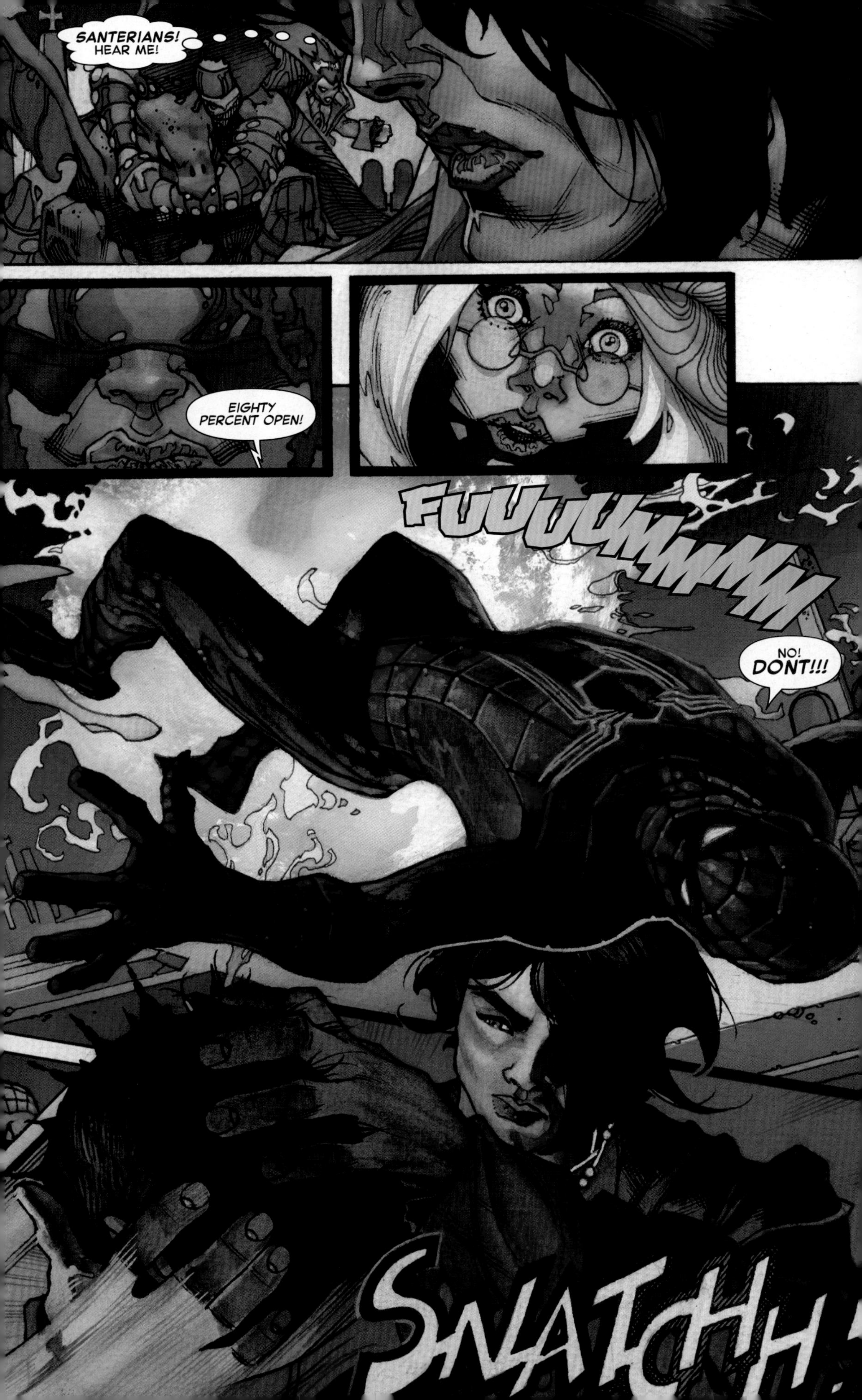
SANTERIANS! HEAR ME!
EIGHTY PERCENT OPEN!
FUUUUMMMM
NO! DONT!!!
SNATCHH!

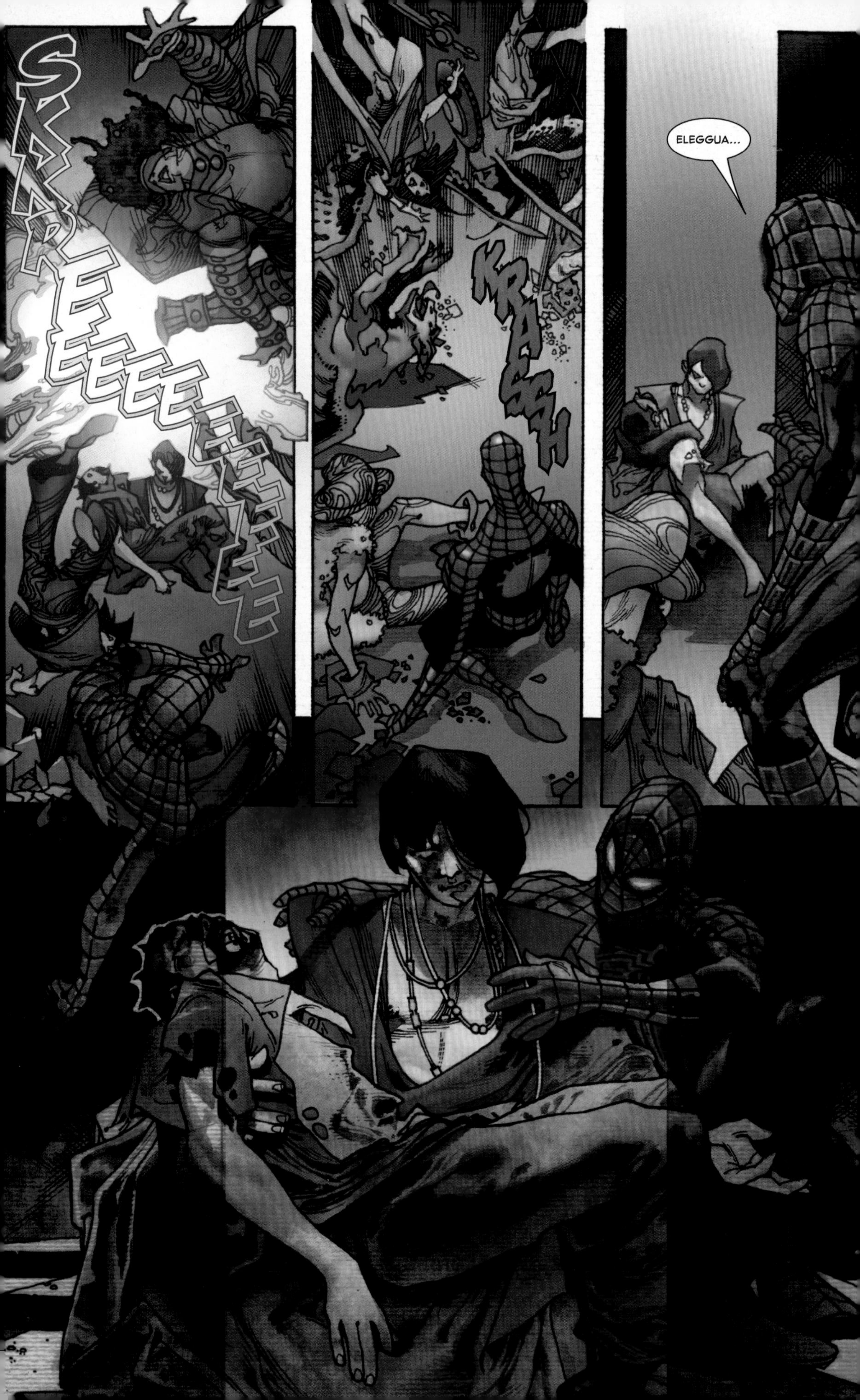
SKRAEEEEEEEEEEE
KRASSSH
ELEGGUA...

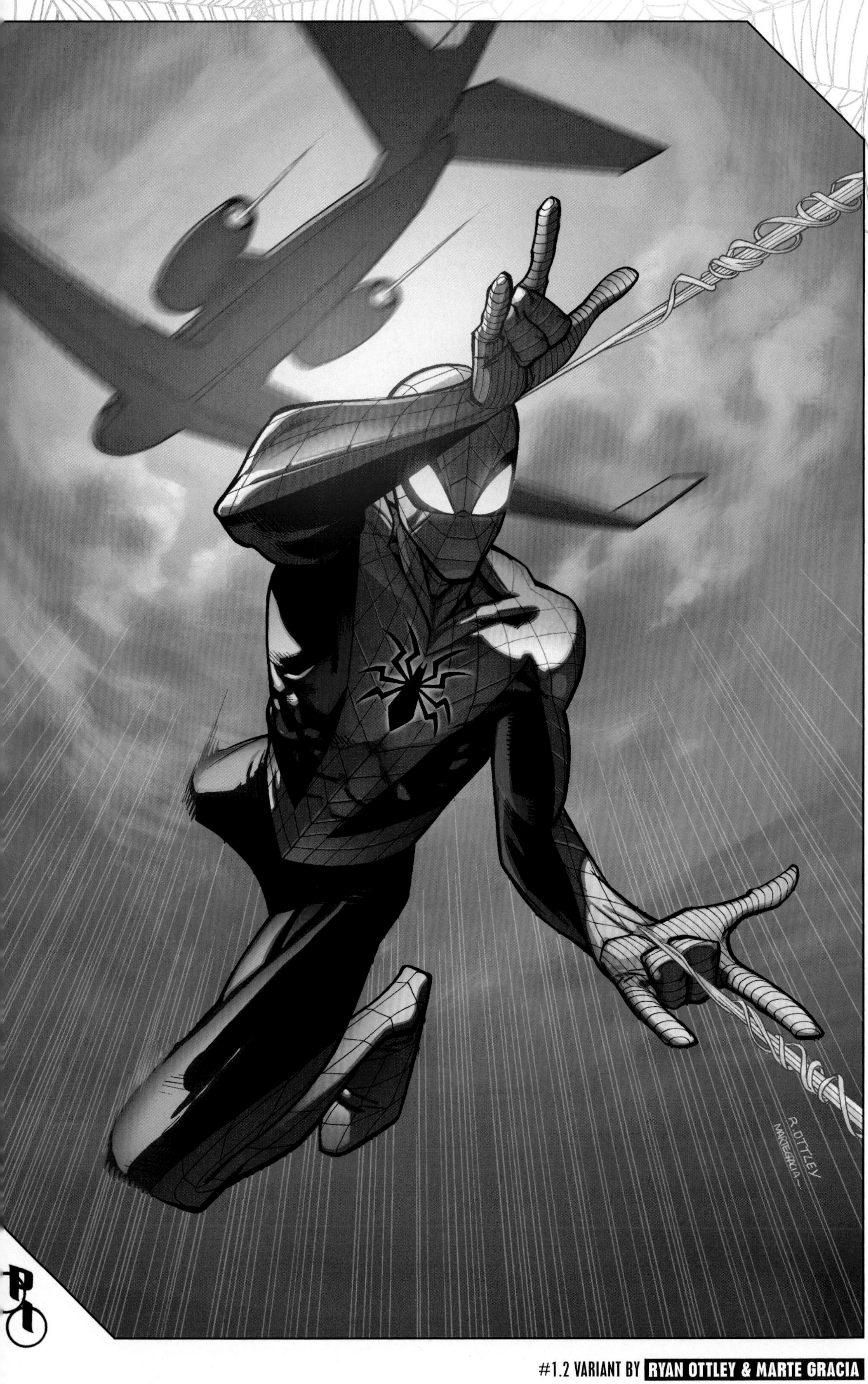
R. OTTLEY

#1.2 VARIANT BY **RYAN OTTLEY & MARTE GRACIA**

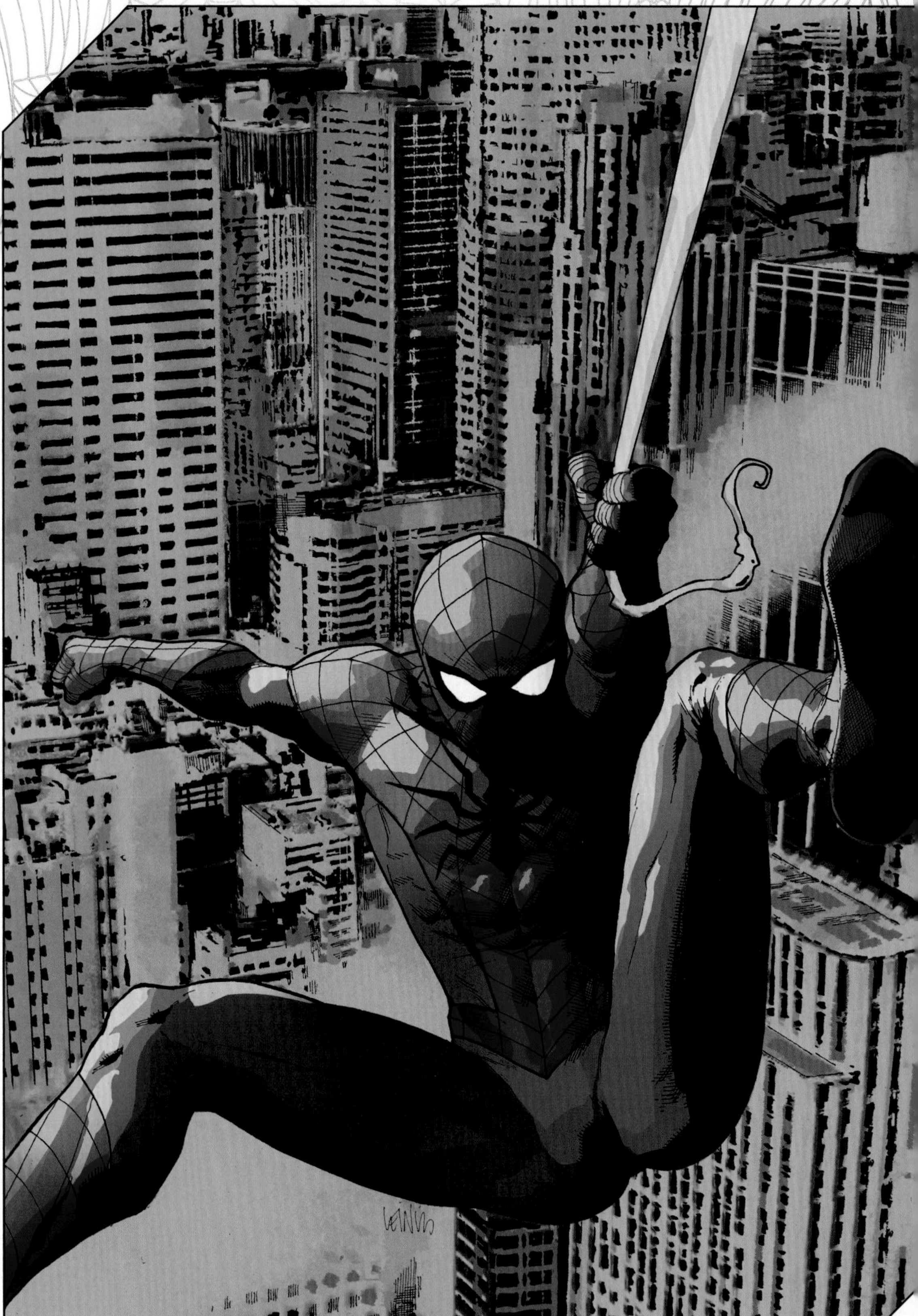

#1.3 VARIANT BY **LEINIL FRANCIS YU**

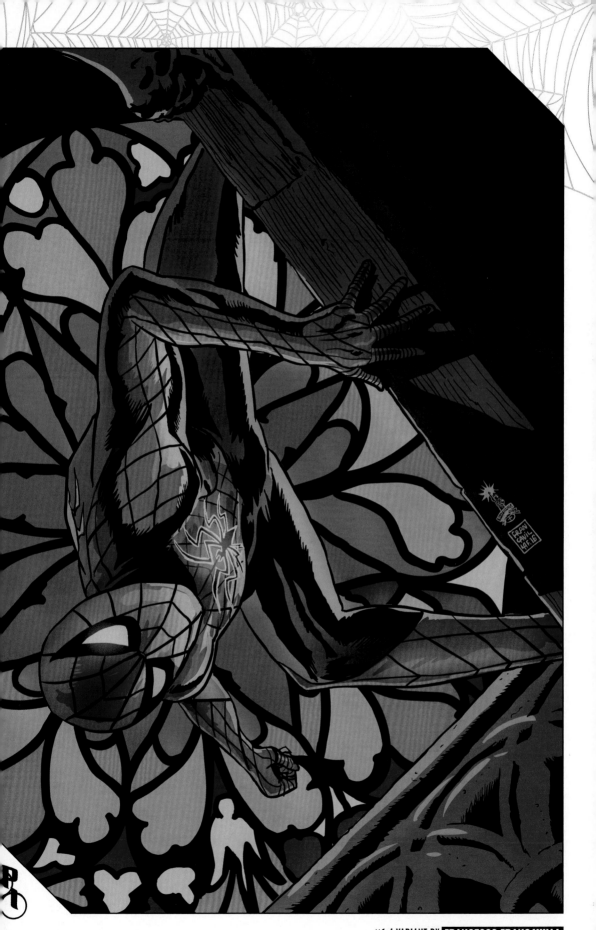

#1.4 VARIANT BY **FRANCESCO FRANCAVILLA**

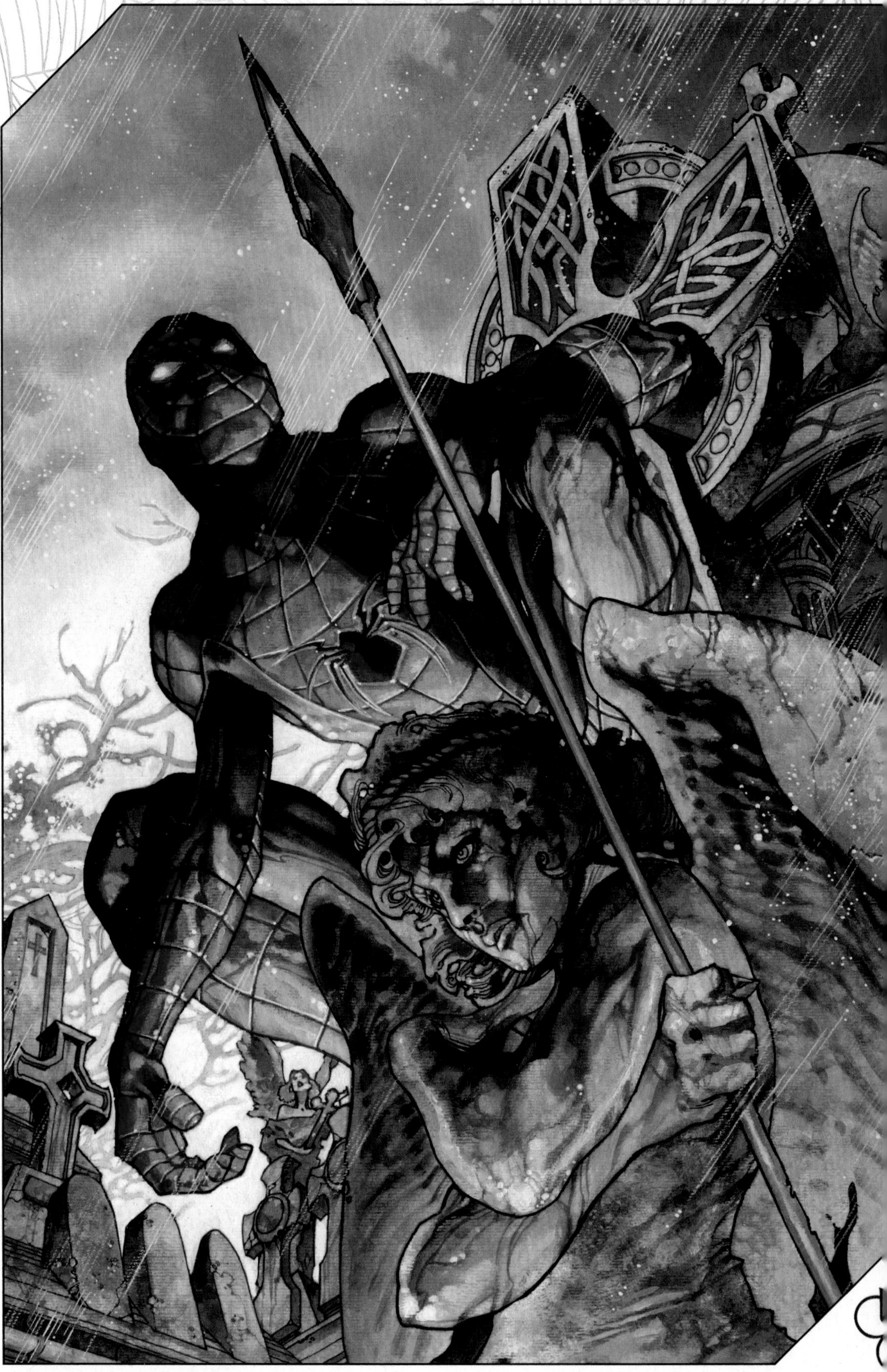

#1.6 VARIANT BY **SIMONE BIANCHI**